33 Day Family Consecration

A Guide for Parents to Total Consecration to Jesus through Mary

BROUSSARD PRESS
Round Rock, Texas

Cover: Bartolomé Esteban Murillo, *The Heavenly and Earthly Trinities*, ca. 1675-82 The National Gallery, London. Used with Permission.

Cover page, Week I: Isabel Burke, *Sts. Joachim and Anne*. Watercolor on paper. Private Collection.

Cover page, Week II: Isabel Burke, *The Annunciation*. Watercolor on paper. Private Collection.

Cover page, Week III: Isabel Burke, *At the Foot of the Cross*. Watercolor on paper. Private Collection.

Cover page, Week IV: Isabel Burke, *The Assumption: Reunited in Heaven*. Watercolor on paper. Private Collection

Cover page, Week V: Isabel Burke, *The Presentation of Mary*. Watercolor on paper. Private Collection.

Coloring Page Drawings, various pages: R. Miller, Private Collection.

First Edition
Copyright © August 2015   Broussard Press
1-713-701-7007 • www.BroussardPress.com
ISBN 978-0-9965980-0-2
Printed in the United States of America

*The Mission of the Family is to
Guard, Reveal, and Communicate Love*

TABLE OF CONTENTS

WEEK I
THE IMMACULATE CONCEPTION AND
OUR CALL TO ADORE GOD

WEEK II
THE ANNUNCIATION: A MYSTERY OF FAITH

WEEK III
MARY AT THE FOOT OF THE CROSS AND
THE MYSTERY OF CHARITY

WEEK IV
THE ASSUMPTION OF MARY AND HOW WE LIVE IN HOPE

WEEK V
THE PRESENTATION OF MARY IN THE TEMPLE -
ICON OF CONSECRATION

RESOURCES FOR FAMILY LIFE

Acknowledgements

This book is a result of inspiration from the Holy Spirit and guidance from our Blessed Mother. I began writing this book during a renewal of our own family consecration to Jesus through Mary using Fr. Nathan Cromly's *Totus Tuus: A Contemplative Guide to Total Consecration to Jesus through Mary* as our guide. Without *Totus Tuus,* this book would not have come to be. So, first of all, we would like to thank Fr. Nathan for his encouragement, enthusiasm, and contributions to this project. Next, I would like to thank my wife Denae and our children who were the first reviewers of these reflections. They provided much feedback and encouragement during our 33 days of family renewal and prayer.

We couldn't have done this project alone, and there are many people who helped us along the way, especially the following:

Those families who participated in our 33 day family consecration pilot group:

Abigail and Jerry Ahrens, Shawna and Scott Aubin, Jessica and Jeff Chaumont, Erin and Aaron Cromly, Jennifer and Joe Fulwiler, Jeanette and Edmund Gieske, Sharon and Adam Gretencord, Deborah and Jason Haney, Anna and Andy Meadows, Katie and Devin Rose, and Becky and Tony Saucedo.

Isabel Burke and her father Gibbons for the beautiful artwork used at the beginning of each week of the consecration. *www.Instagram.com/the.flightless.artist*

R. Miller for creating almost 40 coloring pages so the youngest members of our families can participate also. *www.ImmaculateHeartColoringPages.wordpress.com*

Foreword

"The family that prays together, stays together."
    – Servant of God Patrick Peyton, C.S.C.

"Why should our family make a consecration together?" I wonder if we could not rather ask: why wouldn't your family make a family consecration together? Everyone wants to speak to the members of your family – from rock stars to media pundits to salesmen on TV. Why not give Jesus and Mary their fair turn? Letting God into your family will not take anything away from your family. God does not take anything away from a family. He gives it everything it needs, instead!

Making a personal consecration of oneself to God is an act of devotion whereby a person renews the promises of his Baptism. Making this consecration according to the spirit of St. Louis de Montfort means entrusting the Baptismal promises, whereby one is committed to God, to the heart of the Blessed Virgin Mary. For de Montfort, the secret to living out the grace of Baptism – and, therefore, our entire Christian life – as perfectly and intensely as possible is Mary. By entrusting everything we are to her (something commonly called "consecrating ourselves to her"), we invite her to teach us and help us to grow in faith, hope, and love in and with her.

What does it mean to make this consecration as a family? It means time spent together, sharing about meaningful things. It means children discovering parents as guides on the pathway to God. It means brothers and sisters listening to each other and learning from each other. It means God blessing and protecting you. In brief, it means holiness, unity, and the discovery of God's plan for your family. Again, why not make this consecration? What could be more important than praying together?

I pray that this consecration yields abundant fruits for your family, and, through your family, for the Church. May it inspire harvesters for the Lord's harvest!

In Mary,

Father Nathan Cromly, csj

Editor of *Totus Tuus: A Contemplative Approach to Total Consecration to Jesus through Mary.*

A Word from the Author

*T*his work is the fruit of over twenty years of parenting, cultivated by fifteen years spent in Catholic school and college. It also stems from the many prayers of my relatives who gave up much to ensure that I would receive, embrace, and live out my Catholic faith.

In this book we strive to equip today's parents to pass on the faith to their families effectively, not just as head knowledge, but heart knowledge. The Catholic faith is more than a set of beliefs and moral rules, it is a relationship with Jesus. The mission of *Your Holy Family Ministries* is to provide practical tools to help parents raise saints, missionaries, and martyrs. Our goal is to not be happy with the status quo, but to raise our children to be saints for the new millennium.

A holy family is composed of parents who have a strong personal relationship with the Lord and each have chosen to make Jesus the Lord of their lives. In addition, the marriage is one solidly built on Christian morality, while following God's plan for marriage. With this solid foundation of a personal relationship with the Lord and a marriage striving for God's plan, a holy family is founded. The parents are now equipped to give the gift of faith to their children both by their example and by sharing their knowledge of the Lord within their family.

Through the writings of St. John Paul II and the writings of other holy men and women, we have discovered four areas in which the family can engage to achieve holiness. The first is family prayer, which is why this book has been written. This is the most important part of a holy family. Think of prayer as the oxygen which gives and sustains our very family life. Second is family play, which is a necessity for humans. Family play is an important ingredient in a healthy family life, and is fertile ground for family prayer. We have learned that the better the human relationships are amongst the members of your family, the easier and more fruitful the family prayer life will be.

Family prayer and family play are two essential components of a holy family and will lead to a deeper engagement of each family member within the life of the family. This is our real goal, for the family to be fully alive. The family is your refuge from the world when you have a bad day, a place where you can go and know that you are loved no matter what. John Paul II referred to this state as a communion of persons.

The third area is the engagement of each person with the other members of the family. We focus on equipping the family to be present to each other. A family is meant to be an intimate communion of persons who love each other with the love that God has for us. God's love does not place conditions, it is not fleeting, or nor is it selfish. God's love is strong enough to overcome any obstacle, even when that love is rejected.

Fourth, once we have become a family after God's own heart, we must share this beauty with others in our community. Our job as parents is much easier when we have support from other families in our community who also wish to have Jesus as the Lord of their family.

The mission of the family is to guard, reveal and communicate love. For it is with love that we can change the world one family at a time.

Allen A. Hébert - Co-Founder, Your Holy Family Ministries

Introduction

$\mathcal{T}$hese reflections are intended to be a companion to the book edited by Fr. Nathan Cromly, *Totus Tuus: A Contemplative Approach to Total Consecration to Jesus through Mary.*

Many people have completed a 33 day preparation for total consecration to Jesus through Mary, yet they may not know how to share this beautiful spiritual exercise with their whole family. This series of reflections is our attempt to help you make it accessible to even the younger members of your family. We have targeted these reflections towards anyone over the age of six. For those families who have children who are younger than seven, you may wish to also use Your Holy Family's *33 Day Family Consecration Coloring Book.* The coloring pages in our book match the theme of each day of the consecration, and enable the younger members of your family to participate in the family consecration at their level. The coloring book is available in printed format or can be downloaded from our website.

Why is the consecration 33 days long?

Perhaps it is because Jesus lived on this earth for 33 years and the consecration gives us the opportunity to consecrate our lives to Jesus with one day for each year of his life.

What if I miss a day?

Don't fret about it. God knows the intentions of our hearts. He wants you and your family to grow closer to Him, and dedicating time each day to Him in prayer is a great way to accomplish this. If you miss a day, double up the next day, if you desire, and press on. Don't stop, but try to plan ahead on your family calendar to ensure that nothing gets in the way. Make the daily consecration time a priority-- like eating or sleeping. Daily prayer is essential to your spiritual life, as necessary to our survival as food and drink.

What if my children won't sit still and listen?

Our goal is not to have the children sit still and listen to every word. The words of the companion reflections are merely a means to communicate a piece of the beauty of God's plan for salvation to our children. You do not need to read every word to them. Your goal should be to engage your children in dialog about the topic of the day and to help them build their relationship with God and with the others members of your family (especially with you as their parents). If the children have even one topic that they connect with, and you are able to share in a conversation with them about the beauty of your faith, you have succeeded. Our Lady will take your efforts and multiply them beyond your own abilities.

How to use this guide:

Use Fr. Nathan Cromly's *Totus Tuus: A Contemplative Approach to Total Consecration to Jesus through Mary* as your primary text for the consecration. It is suitable for adults and older teens able to go deeper into the mystery of God. Each week has a theme, and the daily prayers and practices are related to that theme.

The best way to make this consecration something the whole family will benefit from, as well as enjoy, is to set a regular time each day for the whole family to come together and have consecration time. We have found that twenty minutes is sufficient to complete the prayers and reflections, and allow time for a family discussion of the topic of the day. Ideally, one or both parents will read the *Totus Tuus* reflections prior to daily family consecration time. You may also wish to find a time when the adults and teens can sit down and go through the daily reflections in *Totus Tuus*. The reflections in our companion are purposely short and will focus on the main aspect of each daily topic. The *33 Day Family Consecration* should be used as your primary text during the family consecration prayer time, using your family Bible and Fr. Nathan's *Totus Tuus* for the scripture readings and daily closing prayers.

Success Criteria

*W*hen beginning a program like this, many people set the bar way too high. When they fail to achieve that level of perfection, they simply give up. The tips below will provide some advice on how to avoid this trap. The goal is to bring your family closer to God and closer to each other than before the consecration began.

How do I measure our success in this Family Consecration?

- **Your family prayed together more than you did before.** Ideally, you would be coming together in prayer as a family each day for 33 days in a row. But if you miss a day, or have to pray your consecration prayers apart from your family, that is okay. Just do your best, ask Mary to intercede on your behalf, and make the days when your family prays together outnumber the days when you are apart during the daily consecration times.

- **You engaged in a conversation about your faith with your children.** Each day is an opportunity to discuss matters of faith with your children and your spouse. Don't expect that each day you will discover something new and exciting about your faith and have a lively in-depth discussion about it. Rejoice, instead, in those times when your 7 or 8 year old asks you to explain something that you read together. You may even have a few days that really inspire your teenagers to go deeper in their faith, even if they won't openly admit it.

- **On day 34, you attended Mass together as a family, stayed after Mass was over, and prayed the Consecration.** The goal of these 33 days is to prepare each member of your family to consecrate themselves to Jesus through Mary. You as a family are doing this individual consecration together. Even if you miss a day or two, or more, if you come together at the end and consecrate yourselves to Jesus through Mary, you have achieved something wonderful. You can look forward to the next time you do a family consecration and know that your family will continue to grow in holiness and enter more fully into your consecration with each time of renewal.

Getting Started

1. Pick a date to start your preparation for Consecration. For a list of proposed dates, see the Consecration Calendar in this book.

2. Talk with your family about the Consecration a few days before you begin.

   - Give them the big picture, the reasons why you are going to consecrate your family to Jesus through Mary.

     - The reasons will vary, but here are some suggestions:

       - Mary is our Mother, and we love her and her Son; this is a way to show Jesus and Mary that we love them.

       - Scripture tells us to pray without ceasing, and we will practice this as a family over the next 33 days.

       - We need to pray more as a family and this is a great way to start.

       - Our prayers are even stronger when we pray together as a family.

       - It will make your mother happy.

       - We are uniting our prayers for (insert one or more family members or friends who need your prayers).

   - Let them know what to expect each day, what time and how long the daily prayers will take.

     - Read the "How to Use This Book" section in Fr. Nathan's *Totus Tuus*.

3. What to do each day:
   - Make the sign of the Cross to begin your family prayer time.
   - Open with the daily prayer for the given week. (You may wish to make copies of the daily prayer for each week, and let each child in your family who is old enough to read have a copy so you can recite it together.)
   - Review the daily practice for the week; see how everyone is doing with it.
   - Read the daily scripture and explain any parts of the passage which the younger children might not understand. You should stop reading in order to explain or ask questions of the children if you think they may be losing interest. Taking breaks for explanations helps make the scripture come alive for younger listeners.
   - Some families will have one of the children read the scripture aloud. It may help both the young listeners and the child picked to read if he or she practices any difficult words in the passage with a parent beforehand, lest the other members of the family become distracted and perhaps not even listen to the scripture. (Letting the children read may make it more difficult for a parent to pause the reading and answer questions or provide additional insight into the passage.)
   - Discuss the daily reflection. Depending on your level of comfort, you may read the daily reflection from *Totus Tuus* privately and then share a summary with your younger children during this time, or use the reflections in this book to help you share the main points with your family. If you have both older and younger children, the older ones may learn more about the mystery of Marian Consecration by

reading the original reflections in *Totus Tuus* instead of the reflections in this book. **DO NOT** simply give your reading-age children the reflections in this book to read on their own. These reflections are an aid for you to make the Consecration more accessible to your children so that you, as a family, can prepare together. The goal of this program is to help your family to grow closer to the Lord as well as one another.

- Pray the closing prayer.

4. Other Considerations:

- Daily Consecration prayer duration:

  - You should allow for about 20 minutes each day for the consecration. (On the first day of each week, you will read both the introduction to each week and the first day's meditations, so this day will be a little bit longer than the rest of the week. Budget about 30 minutes for the first day of each week.)

- What time of the day works best for the consecration?

  - Pick a time that works for your family - a time when you are not rushed, that will not be cancelled due to other commitments. Pick a time when you won't have to work too hard to keep your commitment.

  - Many families find that right after the family dinner or just before bedtime works well for the consecration; for some families, mornings will work better. The main thing is that the time you select works with your family's schedule.

Suggested Schedules for Consecration

1st. Day	33rd. Day	Consecration Day	
Nov. 29	Dec. 31	**Jan. 1**	Solemnity of Mary, Mother of God
Dec. 6	Jan. 7	**Jan. 8**	Our Lady of Prompt Succor
Dec. 31	Feb. 1	**Feb. 2**	The Purification of the Virgin Mary
Jan. 9	Feb. 10	**Feb. 11**	Our Lady of Lourdes
Feb. 20	Mar. 24	**Mar. 25**	The Annunciation
Mar. 24	Apr. 25	**Apr. 26**	Our Lady of Good Counsel
Mar. 26	Apr. 27	**Apr. 28**	Feast of St. Louis de Montfort
Mar. 29	Apr. 30	**May 1**	Queen of Heaven
Apr. 10	May 12	**May 13**	Our Lady of Fatima
Apr. 28	May 30	**May 31**	The Visitation
May 7	June 8	**June 9**	Mary, Mother of Grace
May 25	June 26	**June 27**	Our Mother of Perpetual Help
May 30	July 1	**July 2**	The Visitation of Our Lady
June 13	July 15	**July 16**	Our Lady of Mount Carmel
July 13	Aug. 14	**Aug. 15**	The Assumption
July 20	Aug. 21	**Aug. 22**	The Queenship of Mary
Aug. 6	Sept. 7	**Sept. 8**	Birth of the Virgin Mary
Aug. 10	Sept. 11	**Sept. 12**	The Most Holy Name of Mary
Aug. 13	Sept. 14	**Sept. 15**	Our Lady of Sorrows
Sept. 4	Oct. 6	**Oct. 7**	Our Lady of the Rosary
Sept. 13	Oct. 15	**Oct. 16**	Purity of the Blessed Virgin Mary
Oct. 14	Nov. 15	**Nov. 16**	Our Lady of Mercy
Oct. 19	Nov. 20	**Nov. 21**	Presentation of the Blessed Virgin Mary
Nov. 5	Dec. 7	**Dec. 8**	The Immaculate Conception
Nov. 9	Dec. 11	**Dec. 12**	Our Lady of Guadalupe

Sts. Anne and Joachim

First Week
The Immaculate Conception and Our Call to Adore God

*I*n this first week of the *Totus Tuus* Consecration we think about the mystery of the Conception of Mary without original sin.

What is Conception?

Conception is the time when a baby is first alive in his or her Mother's womb. This occurs about nine months before a baby is born and everyone else gets to meet him or her.

Mary's parents, St. Anne and St. Joachim, waited a long, long time to have children. They were good, holy people who lived holy lives and, as legend has it, were not able to conceive any children until late in their lives. St. Anne prayed fervently to God for a child and promised to dedicate that child to God if, indeed, they were blessed with one. In the Jewish culture, being infertile (unable to have any children) was considered a curse from God.

Anne and Joachim were very happy when they finally did get pregnant with Mary. As Catholics, we believe that at the moment of conception in St. Anne's womb, Mary was brought into this world without original sin. Original sin is a mystery that we cannot fully understand.

Original sin is not a personal fault or sin; the world has been wounded by Adam and Eve's original sin. Sin is everywhere in the world, and so it is easy for us to sin too. This inclination to sin is known as "concupiscence." In

Baptism, original sin is taken away and we are brought back to God, but after Baptism we are still subject to temptation.

Because God selected Mary to be the mother of His Son, Jesus, He gave Mary the same gift that He gave to Adam and Eve. He gave her freedom from original sin, the opportunity to be perfect and not be inclined to sin, just like Adam and Eve before the fall. Adam and Eve were tempted by the devil and sinned; Mary was surely tempted in her life too, but she chose to obey God in all things and so remained sinless.

Have you ever felt like doing something bad? and even though you knew it was wrong you did it anyway?

That is an example of original sin in your heart. Since Mary was born without original sin, she rarely or never thought about doing something bad like we sometimes do.

This was a great gift from God to Mary, and she responded by glorifying God and following His commands all her life. Mary was open to all that God called her to do, the easy and the difficult, and gave glory to God always.

How do we respond to God's gifts to us? Do we give God glory in all things?

One very good way to glorify God and give Him the praise and honor due to Him is through Adoration. Adoration can be a simple action that acknowledges God's power and glory. You can also visit a Eucharistic chapel and adore Jesus in the Blessed Sacrament. You can find nearby parishes that have hours of Adoration at: www.TheRealPresence.org.

Daily Pious Practice this Week

Make a personal act of adoration three times each day. Just take a moment to recognize God as your Father and Lord. This prayer of adoration may be new to you. We are used to making prayers thanking God for something or asking Him for something, but this prayer just gives Him glory while we are not asking Him for anything in return.

Here are some examples (just to get you thinking of how you can adore the Lord in your own words):

- When you wake up, fold your hands in prayer and say, "Blessed be God, the Lord of the Universe."

- At lunch, open your hands like you are receiving a present and say, "Thank you Lord for this day and this food, praise and glory to You alone."

- At bedtime, bow your head and say, "Praise the Lord for helping me through another day, blessed be the name of the Lord."

Prayer to recite every day of this Week

The Magnificat

My soul proclaims the greatness of the Lord,
my spirit rejoices in God my Savior
for he has looked with favor on his lowly servant.
From this day all generations will call me blessed:
the Almighty has done great things for me,
and holy is his Name.
He has mercy on those who fear him
in every generation.
He has shown the strength of his arm,
he has scattered the proud in their conceit.
He has cast down the mighty from their thrones,
and has lifted up the lowly.
He has filled the hungry with good things,
and the rich he has sent away empty.
He has come to the help of his servant Israel
for he has remembered his promise of mercy,
the promise he made to our fathers,
to Abraham and his children for ever.

- Traditional Catholic Prayer

First Day

Pray the Magnificat

Mary, Mother of Mercy

Scripture reading from the Gospel of **John 8:2-11**[*]
– *The story of the woman caught in adultery*

What did Jesus write in the dirt?

While the words that Christ wrote in the sand are not recorded in sacred scripture, many theologians believe that Jesus was writing the sins of the people who were about to stone the woman.

The Father's Mercy for Mary

God loves us so much. We see this love through our parents. Mercy is God's love shown in a special way when we sin against Him or our neighbor and He continues to love us and forgive our sins. Jesus encountered a group of people condemning a woman for her sins. They looked to him for his approval, but instead, he told them that the one who had no sin should throw the first stone at the woman. No one was without sin, so one by one, they went away. Jesus told the woman that he didn't condemn her either (even though he had no sin and could have cast the first stone), and told her to go and sin no more.

What is adultery?

It is when a man or a woman pretends to be married to someone he or she is not married to.

---

[*] For the scripture passage, please use your family Bible or Fr. Nathan's *Totus Tuus.*

What do you think of God's endless mercy? Would you be able to forgive so completely?

If someone hurt you, would you be able or willing to forgive him as readily as Jesus forgave the woman?

Jesus tells us to "go and sin no more" when we go to the sacrament of Confession. We examine our conscience and recall all the ways we fall short and disobey God's laws. We approach Him and ask for forgiveness and He does not condemn us, but instead shows us His mercy and tells us to go and sin no more.

What is a conscience?

Everyone has a conscience: It is that voice in your mind that helps you choose right from wrong.

How do you fall short of following God's laws? Is going to confession something you like to do?

In the case of Mary's Immaculate Conception, she was saved from the stain of sin before she was born. By thinking about this perfect example of God's mercy for someone as completely human as we are, we can better understand the love God has for each of us. He loved us even while we were sinners, and extends His infinite mercy to each of us as many times as we ask for it.

What does infinite mean?

It means that there is no beginning or end to it. God's mercy has no limit, it will always be there, and we can never use it all up.

Daily Pious Practice Reminder

Make a personal act of adoration three times each day.

Finish up your family consecration time by reciting the closing prayer found in Fr. Nathan's *Totus Tuus*.

— Saint Anne and Saint Joachim —

Second Day

Pray the Magnificat

Mary, Virgin Most Faithful

Scripture reading from **Genesis 3:1-13***
 – *The Serpent in the Garden and the First Sin by Adam
 and Eve.*

**If we were Adam or Eve in the garden, do you think we
would choose to obey God?**

> *Sin is attractive and pleasurable; or we feel pressured
> by "friends" to do something that we know is wrong,
> and many times we do it anyway.*

Responding to the Father's Mercy

In the beginning God made Adam and Eve without sin. But
Adam and Eve didn't fully trust God, and so when the serpent
tempted them, perhaps even threatened them, they chose to
disobey God's one command in the Garden of Eden. They ate
the fruit of the tree of knowledge which God had instructed
them not to eat.

**Why did God tell Adam and Eve not to eat the fruit of the
tree of knowledge?**

> *It may be because God wanted Adam and Eve to trust
> Him completely and learn good and evil from Him
> and Him alone. When they ate the fruit, they could
> determine right and wrong for themselves and make up*

---

* For the scripture passage, please use your family Bible or Fr. Nathan's *Totus Tuus.*

their own ideas of what was right and wrong apart from God.

The choice they made was between perfect Love (God) and their own desires. Their own selfishness won. God loves us so much, and He only wants what is best for us. He wants us to love Him in return, but many times we choose to turn towards ourselves and do what "feels" best, not what God wants.

What does it mean to be selfish?

Being selfish is thinking of yourself first. It is doing something that will make you happy and not worrying about how it may affect others.

Adam and Eve were God's creation, and He knew what would make them happy. His one command not to eat of the tree in the center of the garden was a command of love to protect them from evil, from selfishness.

Adam and Eve allowed themselves to be tempted. They should have called out to God for protection from the serpent, but instead they listened to the serpent and chose to believe his lies. The serpent, otherwise known as the devil, was the first liar. He tells us what we want to hear, and tempts us to distrust and disobey God. He makes sin look fun and enjoyable; it is only after we sin that we discover we were tricked.

In the bible, the Hebrew term for serpent is a bit different from the English word "snake." It means a fierce beast or a very scary monster. So when Adam and Eve encountered the serpent in the garden, they may have been afraid of what the monster might do to them.

What would you do if you encountered a dangerous snake?

*Go to your parents, right? What should Adam and Eve
have done?*

How can we know what God wants us to do?

*We can read scripture, we can spend time in prayer, we
can talk with people we know who are close to God.
Also, examine your conscience daily and receive the
sacraments of Eucharist and Reconciliation often.*

Daily Pious Practice Reminder

Make a personal act of adoration three times each day.

**Finish up your family consecration time by reciting
the closing prayer found in Fr. Nathan's *Totus Tuus.***

THE MERCY OF GOD

Third Day

Pray the Magnificat

Mary the Beloved Daughter of the Father

Scripture reading from the **Song of Songs 2:1-2,4:1a,7,12,15***
– *A Love Song from our God to His beloved: each of us.*

Mary, Masterpiece of God's Mercy

The Immaculate Conception is God's Masterpiece of Mercy. He made Mary perfect, free from all sin, just as He did when He created Adam and Eve. He gives us a similar gift through Baptism. In Baptism, we are washed free from original sin and we are made new.

Who is the Immaculate Conception?

Mary. She was conceived without sin in the womb of her mother, St. Anne.

What is innocence?

Innocence is the state of having done nothing wrong, nothing to be ashamed of.

The Immaculate Conception stops sin before it starts, contains sin and prevents it from ever touching Mary. Adam and Eve, through sin, distorted God's masterpiece, but God created a new masterpiece in Mary, the first of the redeemed. We are her children and we are redeemed through the blood of the Cross and the grace of Baptism.

---

* For the scripture passage, please use your family Bible or Fr. Nathan's *Totus Tuus.*

Is it better to fall into the mud and then take a bath, or never to fall into the mud in the first place?

Of course it is better to never fall into the mud. But if we do get muddy, then we are thankful for the opportunity to take a bath. The spiritual analogy is that Mary never falls into the mud, which is sin, but we do. Through baptism we are made clean, and then we have the sacrament of reconciliation to cleanse us on a regular basis afterwards.

If Mary is the new Eve, created without sin, who is the new Adam?

Jesus is the new Adam, fully God and fully man, without the stain of original sin. This is a mystery, but Jesus is truly man, so he is the new Adam, a man without original sin and in perfect union with God the Father.

Daily Pious Practice Reminder

Make a personal act of adoration three times each day.

Finish up your family consecration time by reciting the closing prayer found in Fr. Nathan's *Totus Tuus*.

THE FALL OF ADAM AND EVE

Fourth Day

Pray the Magnificat

Mary, Virgin Most Pure

Scripture Reading from **1 John 2:28 – 3:3**[*]
– We are children of God and God is a loving Father.

Wrapped in the Father's Mercy

God chose Mary to be the mother of His Son. Mary is
merely a human being just like us, and God showed great love
for us by choosing a human being to be the mother of His Son.
Mary didn't do anything to deserve this great gift. We haven't
done anything to deserve God's love either, but He gave it to us
anyway, asking us only to love Him in return.

Who else loves you, no matter what (unconditionally)?

*Answers may include parents, brothers and sisters, and
extended family, parish priests, members of a religious
community, the bishop.*

**What does it mean to love someone? How do you know
someone loves you?**

*It means to desire the very best for that person. Loving
someone is helping him or her to grow closer to God
and to obey His commands, because it is by following
God's commands that we will be truly happy.*

God loves us with a never ending love that is not dependent
on whether or not we love Him in return. Like the father

---

[*] For the scripture passage, please use your family Bible or Fr. Nathan's *Totus Tuus.*

in the story of the prodigal son, He is always watching and waiting for us to return to Him. When we return, He is ready to welcome us back, reconcile with us, and love us as if we had never done anything wrong in the first place.

When we remain in God's love, we can be confident that we are pleasing God, our Father. Being faithful to God's commands helps us to live without fear or shame. Mary had complete confidence in God and His faithfulness to her. The Immaculate Conception bestowed this original innocence upon her relationship with God. In Mary's heart there is complete trust that God loves her and wants only what is best for her.

What can we do to be merciful to others like God the Father is merciful to us?

Always be ready to forgive when people hurt us. Do not hold grudges.

Why do you think God chose Mary to be the mother of His son?

Mary didn't do anything to cause God to choose her, God's choice was a complete gift to her. However, her parents did respond to God's love by dedicating Mary to God's service, and Mary only wished to serve God with her whole heart. God gives us gifts and if we are prepared, we can joyfully receive them as Mary did.

Daily Pious Practice Reminder

Make a personal act of adoration three times each day.

Finish up your family consecration time by reciting the closing prayer found in Fr. Nathan's *Totus Tuus*.

Fifth Day

Pray the Magnificat

Mary, Model of Holiness

Scripture Reading from the book of **Wisdom 7:22-27**[*]
– Wisdom is the model of holiness

Who in scripture prayed for wisdom and it was granted to him?

King Solomon, who is considered the author of the book of Wisdom.

Mary, Masterpiece of Creation

The Immaculate Conception is not just for us to admire (like a beautiful painting), but for us to study and imitate. There are many beautiful things we see on a daily basis, like the latest expensive electronic gadgets, expensive sports cars, beautiful artwork, and all we can do is admire them. For most of us, there is no way we can ever hope to obtain these things for ourselves.

What is beautiful to you? Is it someone you know? a car, something in nature, something at Mass?

The Immaculate Conception (Mary) is different. Mary is God's masterpiece that He gives to us, not just for us to look at, but for us to imitate. Mary was given this gift of being immaculate (perfectly sinless) at one point in time, the very moment of her creation. We, born into sin, enter into

---

[*] For the scripture passage, please use your family Bible or Fr. Nathan's *Totus Tuus.*

perfection gradually, but the end God desires for each of us is the same, eternal perfection with Him in Heaven.

God could have made us all perfect instantly, but He chose to lead us through a process of becoming perfect following Mary, our Mother. Mary is our model, the goal we wish to achieve. With God's help we can truly make Mary our model.

What can we do to have a soul that is clean like Mary's? What is the quickest way for us to become holy like her?

Dedicate your life to serving God completely.

Pray, fast, and give your money away to the poor (Tobit 12:8-9, 1 Corinthians 7:3-5, Luke 2:37, Luke 12:33).

Daily Pious Practice Reminder

Make a personal act of adoration three times each day.

Finish up your family consecration time by reciting the closing prayer found in Fr. Nathan's *Totus Tuus*.

Mary, God's Masterpiece

Sixth Day

Pray the Magnificat

Mary, Our Mother

Scripture Reading from the Gospel of **John 15:12-17**[*]
– *Love one another.*

How much do you love your friends? Would you do anything for them?

All Love is from God

Humility is knowing who we are, and being honest about what we can and can't do. To be humble, we must admit that we are only human and that we are created by God. We must admire the Father because He is God, He is all-powerful, and He knows everything; and, at the same time, we must admit that we are not all powerful and that we don't know everything.

Everything we have, we have because God gave it to us. Whatever talents we have, we have because God gave them to us. We don't have anything that did not come from God.

What talents do you have?

Answers will vary. If a child can't come up with something, other family members may tell them what they think their talents are.

The devil was created by God, but he rejected God's plan of salvation. He admits that God is the creator of all things, but does not accept Him as Father. We must be careful that we

---

* For the scripture passage, please use your family Bible or Fr. Nathan's *Totus Tuus.*

do not fall into the same error as the devil. God is our loving Father, Who gives us gifts for our own good.

God is the cause of our joy, and we must not forget this fact. The Immaculate Conception is a reminder of the great gifts that God has given us, and what He has given to Mary. Even if we make mistakes or experience difficulties, we must not let these things reduce our joy of knowing that God loves us and gives us such great gifts. Mary, and her Immaculate Conception, is a gift from God to each of us (see John 19:27).

It is hard to be joyful all the time; what can we do to always remember that God loves us?

> *We need to adore God daily, acknowledge His goodness, and know that He is our Father and Creator.*

> *The key to happiness is **JOY**–Jesus first, **O**thers second, Yourself last.*

How can we show that we love our neighbor?

> *We can show our love for our neighbor by acts of kindness – bringing meals to the sick and suffering, helping someone with his homework, doing yard work for a neighbor, giving compliments, and thanking people for their acts of kindness.*

How can we be more humble?

> *Adore God daily, be thankful for all the gifts we have been given, serve others by putting them before ourselves and our needs.*

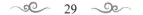

Daily Pious Practice Reminder

Make a personal act of adoration three times each day.

Finish up your family consecration time by reciting the closing prayer found in Fr. Nathan's *Totus Tuus*.

All Love Is From God

Seventh Day

Pray the Magnificat

Mary, Chosen by God

Scripture Reading from **Song of Songs 4:7-12 & 6:3,9-10***
– *We are perfect in God's eyes.*

Mary, Reflection of the Blessed Trinity

Mary is one of us, a human being just like us, but one who reflects the image of God perfectly. Spiritual writers have used an analogy to describe Mary: The Holy Trinity is the sun and Mary is the moon. The moon does not produce any light by itself, but it does glow when the sun shines on it. The only reason the moon is visible to us is because the sun shines on it and the moon reflects that sunlight.

Mary is a perfect mirror of God. Mary is a beloved daughter of the Father, Son and Holy Spirit.

How well do we reflect the love of God?

It is our goal in life to reflect the love of God in this world as perfectly as possible. One way to do this is follow the commands of the Lord and love one another as God loves us.

---

* For the scripture passage, please use your family Bible or Fr. Nathan's *Totus Tuus.*

Now that we have completed the first week the consecration, what new things have you learned about God through the daily reflections?

The first week of the consecration has focused on taking us deeper into the mystery that is the Immaculate Conception. Name one thing that you learned about the Immaculate Conception that you didn't know before.

Daily Pious Practice Reminder

Make a personal act of adoration three times each day.

Finish up your family consecration time by reciting the closing prayer found in Fr. Nathan's *Totus Tuus*.

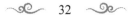

Mary and the Angel Gabriel

Second Week
The Annunciation: A Mystery of Faith

*A*cts of Adoration help us keep our faith pure by keeping our eyes fixed on the Lord. Adoration of God also helps us follow God's commands in a more perfect, loving way, because we realize how much higher God's ways are than our ways, His thoughts than our thoughts (Isaiah 55:9).

How do we know what God's ways are? How can we know His thoughts?

By reading sacred scripture and praying daily, not just talking, but listening to God in our heart.

God loves us so much; how can we respond? We respond to God's love by loving Him more and trusting more in Him. St. Louis de Montfort was a priest who lived in the early 1700s in France. He loved God with his whole heart and was very devoted to our blessed mother Mary. He modeled his life after Mary's, and asked her to help him dedicate his life to God. He wrote many books about how Mary could help everyone love God more perfectly and live their lives dedicated to God.

How can Mary help us to follow God?

We can read about her life and how she lived only for God. We can read about her messages to the world through such Church-approved apparitions as Fatima, Lourdes, Akita,and Guadalupe.

What is an Apparition?

An apparition is a private revelation from heaven to one person or many persons. Sometimes Mary appears to people on earth and gives them a message to help themselves and others of that time to live holier lives dedicated to God. (Mary appeared to Bernadette at Lourdes; Mary appeared to the children at Fatima.)

This second week in our consecration will focus on the Annunciation. We think about the Annunciation in the first Joyful Mystery of the Holy Rosary. It is when the angel Gabriel appeared to Mary and announced to her that she would be the Mother of the Savior, Jesus. Mary's response to Gabriel was, "I am the handmaid of the Lord, let it be done unto me according to thy word." Mary probably didn't fully understand everything the angel told her, but in faith she said yes and continued following God throughout her life.

Do you know that God speaks to you, too?

God speaks to us all the time. We just need to pray to Him and then spend time listening for His reply. Even if we do not hear anything with our ears, we can listen with our hearts and listen to those God has put in our lives to speak to us (our priests, parents, teachers, etc.). He will always guide us to know what we should do, even if He wants us to search for Him sometimes.

Daily Pious Practice this Week

Choose a verse from the Bible to read and think about each day. Print it out or write it down, and place it where you will see it several times a day. You can put it in more than one place (on the fridge door, on your night stand, at your seat at the dining table). If you have difficulty finding a verse that speaks to you or your children, you may wish to consider the following passages which relate to family life:

Joshua 24:15   John 3:16   Matthew 19:14

Prayer to recite every day of this Week

The Angelus

V. The Angel of the Lord declared unto Mary.

R. And she conceived by the Holy Spirit.

Hail Mary, full of grace, the Lord is with thee; blessed art thou among women, and blessed is the fruit of thy womb, Jesus. Holy Mary, Mother of God, pray for us sinners, now and at the hour of our death. Amen.

V. Behold the handmaid of the Lord.

R. Be it done unto me according to thy word.

Hail Mary, etc.

V. And the Word was made Flesh. *(genuflect)*

R. And dwelt among us.

Hail Mary, etc.

V. Pray for us, O holy Mother of God.

R. That we may be made worthy of the promises of Christ.

LET US PRAY

Pour forth, we beseech Thee, O Lord, Thy grace into our hearts, that we, to whom the Incarnation of Christ, Thy Son, was made known by the message of an angel, may, by His Passion and Cross, be brought to the glory of His Resurrection. Through the same Christ Our Lord. Amen.

- Traditional Catholic Prayer

First Day

Pray the Angelus

Mary, Servant of God's Word

Scripture reading from the Gospel of **Luke 1:26-38**[*]
– *The Annunciation*

Imagine yourself praying in your room; suddenly, an angel appears to you with a request from God. Would you be scared, surprised, shocked? Probably all of the above. What would you say to the angel? Would you say yes to the angel's request?

Renewing our Faith

Mary is our model of faith: Her response to the angel, who announced that she would conceive and bear a son who would be the savior of the world, is perfect. Mary spent her whole life preparing for that day. She most likely prayed, read the sacred scriptures, followed God's commandments, and dedicated herself to God's service on a daily basis.

When God speaks to you and asks you to do something great for Him, will you be ready to say 'yes'?

There are many prayers that we recite each day–the Our Father, Hail Mary, Glory Be, and many others–but do we really think about the words that we are saying when we pray these prayers? The Our Father is the prayer that Jesus taught us. It is the perfect prayer for us to pray; but, if we just repeat the words, then we accomplish very little. These prayers are meant to bring us closer to God. We must think about the words we

---

[*] For the scripture passage, please use your family Bible or Fr. Nathan's *Totus Tuus.*

are saying when we pray. The goal is not to quickly recite the
prayers and finish our prayer time. The goal of all our prayers
is to grow in our relationship with God and get to know Him
better.

Who wrote the Hail Mary?

*The angel Gabriel wrote the first part at the
Annunciation, "Hail Mary, full of grace." St.
Elizabeth, inspired by the Holy Spirit, wrote the
second part at the Visitation, "Blessed are you among
women and blessed is the fruit of your womb."
Then the Church added the name of the fruit of her
womb, "Jesus," and continued with a prayer for her
assistance, "Holy Mary, Mother of God, pray for us
sinners now and at the hour of our death, Amen."*

When we pray, we must contemplate the words we are
saying. What does it mean to *contemplate*? It means that we
spend time thinking about the words we are saying, spend
time with God - more than we need to, an excessive amount of
time - just being with God. Our time of prayer is more than us
doing something–talking or reading scripture–we also need to
be quiet and listen for God to speak with us. God is speaking
to each of us all the time, but we spend too much time talking
and not enough time listening.

What is distracting you from hearing God?

*Answers will vary, but common distractions are the TV,
electronics, cell phones, sports, friends, being too busy.*

In our daily life, we seem to want to constantly be
entertained by something. Using TV, music, and games, we are
always trying to break the silence and fill it with noise. How

can God get our attention and tell us what He wants us to hear if we never stop and listen to Him speaking?

Homework:

Write down the Our Father and identify the different parts of the prayer. One part is a prayer of adoration, one part is a prayer of petition, another is praise, and another is intercession. The Our Father is the perfect prayer, the very model of prayer. We can write our own unique prayer based on the parts of the Our Father.

The words of the prayer are important, but the relationship with God is more important. The end goal of all prayer is a better relationship with God. We need to spend time with Him: this is the only way we will build the most important relationship of our life. Then we will be ready to do whatever God is calling us to do. We will be ready to say Yes to God, just like Mary did. She can help you to be ready. Just ask her to show you the way.

Daily Pious Practice Reminder

Read and think about your bible verse.

Finish up your family consecration time by reciting the closing prayer found in Fr. Nathan's *Totus Tuus.*

The Family That Prays Together Stays Together

Second Day

Pray the Angelus

Mary, Mother of Divine Grace

Scripture reading from the Gospel of **John 1:1-14**[*]
– *The Word became flesh.*

Jesus is the Word of God, come down from heaven to teach us about God, to show us how much God loves us. John the Baptist was the last prophet of Israel, who told everyone about Jesus and prepared the way for his coming into the world.

Growing in Faith

What is love? Love is being vulnerable to someone else. When we love, we seek the best for everyone else and think of them before ourselves. Love must also be shared. When we love, we must go out and share that love with the world. God is Love, and it was not enough for God to keep this love to Himself: He sent His Son, Jesus, into the world, as a baby, to show the world love. Love is a gift.

When you love someone do you wish to be with him or her, and to do things with him or her?

Probably yes, we always desire to be with those we love, to show them we love them, and to enjoy their company.

Love can be seen perfectly in the Holy Trinity–Father, Son and Holy Spirit. St. John Paul II wrote extensively about how we can learn more about ourselves by contemplating the

---

[*] For the scripture passage, please use your family Bible or Fr. Nathan's *Totus Tuus.*

mystery of the Trinity. The Trinity shows love perfectly in the love between the Father and Son. The Father gives His love to the Son, and the Son gives His love to the Father, completely. The Love between the Father and the Son is so deep and so perfect because it is bound and sealed by the third person of the Trinity, the Holy Spirit. The Holy Trinity is a mystery we will never fully understand. St. Patrick used a three-leaf clover to show how the Father, Son, and Holy Spirit are one God but three Persons. This analogy is not perfect, but it helps us to understand better. Don't worry if you don't understand completely, just ask God to help you understand better.

Do you love your parents? Your brothers and sisters, your grandparents? How do you show that love?

It is hard to be generous with your time and your things. What can you do to better love your friends and family?

Try putting others' needs ahead of your own. For example, when sitting down to dinner, instead of taking the first serving for yourself, offer it to someone else. It may not be easy the first time, but with practice it will become natural.

The Trinity is a mystery, but one that we can better understand when we look at the love between a man and woman who are married. They love each other so much that this love often results in a another person, a baby. Babies are cute, and also a beautiful, visible sign of the love between a man and woman.

Daily Pious Practice Reminder

Read and think about your bible verse.

Finish up your family consecration time by reciting the closing prayer found in Fr. Nathan's *Totus Tuus*.

Third Day

Pray the Angelus

Mary, Mother of Christ

Scripture reading from the Gospel of **Luke 2:7-19***
– The Nativity

*Imagine yourself in the stable watching Mary and
Joseph with baby Jesus. Then angels start singing, and
the shepherds come by to see the newborn king. The
stable probably smells, it is cold, and yet there is peace.*

Keeping God's Word

In the Annunciation, God shares a secret with Mary. That
secret was that He was sending His Son into the world to
redeem the world, to save the world. How special Mary must
have felt being entrusted with such a beautiful secret. When
God shares a secret it is a bit different than when we share one
with our friends: God's secrets can transform the world!

Mary kept this secret safe for thirty years. She knew her
son was the savior, but she couldn't tell anyone. Probably
not many people would have believed her anyway. In fact,
very few people believed Jesus when he told them he was the
Messiah. According to sacred scripture, Mary did not even tell
Joseph her secret (but an angel did, and only then did Joseph
take Mary into his home).

---

* For the scripture passage, please use your family Bible or Fr. Nathan's *Totus Tuus.*

Has anyone ever told you a secret that was really important? How did that make you feel?

We must be like a child, completely trusting in our heavenly Father in order to receive this gift which is now given to the entire world. Many people who met Jesus in person were not able to receive this gift because their faith was not childlike. Not much has changed today; many reject the Good News, the Gospel of Jesus Christ, because they think they know better, or they consider themselves to be too wise to believe in a God they cannot see.

How can you share God's secret with the world?

Jesus is Lord and He loves us. He died, He rose from the dead, and He lives forever.

How does it make you feel when someone you love doesn't accept the secret when you tell him or her?

What responsibility do we have since we have been told this secret?

We are to share this Good News with everyone we meet.

Daily Pious Practice Reminder

Read and think about your bible verse.

Finish up your family consecration time by reciting the closing prayer found in Fr. Nathan's *Totus Tuus*

Fourth Day

Pray the Angelus

Mary, Beloved of God

Scripture Reading from **Song of Songs 2:3-10**[*]
– *Longing for God*

*This scripture passage is very beautiful and tells the
story of a very intense love between two people. This
love story is how God loves us and wishes for us to
love Him in return. Some of the imagery may be
too abstract for younger members of the family to
understand, so feel free to shorten the passage or use
words that may be more accessible for your family.*

Offering our Hearts to the Father

At the Annunciation, when Mary gave her "Yes" to God,
it was the perfect yes, or *fiat*, to God. It serves as the perfect
example of how we should respond to God's invitation to
follow Him completely, to offer our lives completely in service
to God.

What is a fiat?

*Fiat literally means, "Let it be done." This was Mary's
response to the angel Gabriel at the Annunciation.*

Mary's fiat is more than just a one time answer to the
angel's message: it was how she lived her whole life. She
continued to say to God, "Let it be done according to Your
will," her whole life. Mary's fiat was the first of many fiats by

---

[*] For the scripture passage, please use your family Bible or Fr. Nathan's *Totus Tuus*.

holy men and women who followed in her footsteps, guided by her example of doing whatever God asked of her.

Saying yes to God can be easy, but not always. When have you said yes to God? What can you do to be ready to say yes to God when He asks you to do something that is not what you want to do?

Mary was able to give her fiat because she loved God with all her heart. In response to Mary's fiat, God's love consumed her completely and made her a new creation. Mary's adoration of God enabled her to lead her husband, Joseph, to love God more than he did before. Mary can do the same for us. Her motherly love of us, and her complete dedication to God, helps us to also choose to give our fiat to God. Led and encouraged by Mary, we can dedicate, or consecrate, our lives completely to God and allow Him to make us saints.

Are we inspired to do great things by the example of our parents and grandparents?

Of course we are. When we see those who are older than us, who have lived virtuous lives, continue to choose God even through trials and difficulties, we are inspired to be better than we were yesterday. Mary is the perfect example of living a life dedicated to God, giving her fiat daily and following God completely.

Daily Pious Practice Reminder

Read and think about your bible verse.

Finish up your family consecration time by reciting the closing prayer found in Fr. Nathan's *Totus Tuus*.

Fifth Day

Pray the Angelus

Mary, Cause of our Joy

Scripture Reading from the Gospel of **Luke 1:39-45**[*]
– *The Visitation*

How did Elizabeth know Mary was pregnant?

*Answers may vary, and sacred scripture does not
tell us; but we can infer from the deep prayer life
of Elizabeth and Zechariah that she was probably
prompted by the Holy Spirit to greet Mary in this way.*

Interesting observation: *Jesus blessed John in his
mother's womb, and that may be why John leapt for
joy.*

Serving God in Faith

Mary becomes the servant of God, more than all those who
went before her in the Old Testament, more than Abraham,
Moses, David, or John the Baptist. Her fiat made her the
perfect servant of God. She became the mother of the Savior,
giving Him her flesh and blood; she was "all in."

How much do you want to give in serving God?

*Would you give yourself completely to Him, body and
soul, if He called you to? How much do you want
to give in serving God? Many saints have given all*

---

[*] For the scripture passage, please use your family Bible or Fr. Nathan's *Totus Tuus.*

for God; and Mary surely helped them to make this ultimate sacrifice, to be witnesses to the love of God.

Serving God means being His instrument and doing His work in the world. He wants to work in and through us, to help other people when they need help, and to teach them about who God is and how much He loves all of us. He wants us to help Him! First, we pray in our hearts, "Jesus, I give you everything I am. Do with me whatever You wish for the glory of God the Father." Then, we apply ourselves to whatever Jesus has called us to do, and we try to help those He puts in our path.

Do you believe in God, do you trust in Him completely, are you willing to do anything He asks you to do? If the answer is yes, can you prove it by your actions. Would others be able to look at your life and see enough evidence to prove that you love God with your whole heart?

How can you serve God in your family?

Answers will vary. Serving others in your family. Obeying your parents the first time they ask you to do something or stop doing something. Helping without being asked. Sharing your toys and favorite foods with others.

Mary let God consume her whole life; she was the handmaid of the Lord, and her life and her actions were proof of this.

What do you think God will ask you to do when you grow up?

Daily Pious Practice Reminder

Read and think about your bible verse.

Finish up your family consecration time by reciting the closing prayer found in Fr. Nathan's *Totus Tuus*.

THE VISITATION

Sixth Day

Pray the Angelus

Mary, Beloved of God

Scripture Reading from the Gospel of **Luke 1:46-55***
– *The Magnificat*

When Elizabeth sees Mary, she praises her, rejoicing in how much God has blessed Mary. When Mary hears Elizabeth's praises, she sings a hymn, giving glory to God. How humble this is! Mary recognizes that God has blessed her, and she thanks Him by acknowledging that all of her blessings come from God. We can learn much from Mary's humility.

Keeping a Pure Heart

When grace and charity enter your heart, your heart is purified. When God's grace entered fully into Mary's heart, it preserved her even from any inclination to sin. She is completely full of charity (God's love), which enables her to give herself completely to God and to the child in her womb, Jesus.

What is an inclination?

It is a tendency to like or prefer something.

---

* For the scripture passage, please use your family Bible or Fr. Nathan's *Totus Tuus*.

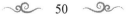

What actions can you do to show your enemies that you love them?

Be kind to them even when they are mean to you. Do something nice for them. Pray for them. Always talk politely about them to others.

Selfishness is a roadblock on our way to God. When we put the needs of others first we begin to love as God loves us.

Daily Pious Practice Reminder

Read and think about your bible verse.

Finish up your family consecration time by reciting the closing prayer found in Fr. Nathan's *Totus Tuus*.

Loving Our Enemies

Seventh Day

Pray the Angelus

Mary, Model of Faith

Scripture Reading from **Genesis 17:1-8 & 15-21***
– *Abraham, our father in faith*

Abraham believed God's promise even though he could not see how God would fulfill it. God gave him a son by his wife Sarah, and they named him Isaac, which means "he laughs." Sometimes we laugh at God's plans, because they seem impossible, but with God all things are possible.

Firm in Faith

Faith is never stagnant. With every choice we make, we either move closer to God or move away from His love. Mary is a model for how our faith can constantly grow and take us closer to God. Fr. Marie-Dominique Philippe, O.P. identifies three stages in Mary's faith journey: Before Jesus, With Jesus, and After Jesus. Regardless of what stage she was in, throughout all of her life, Mary sought to know God's will better and to model her life according to God's plan for her.

What daily choices do we make that bring us closer to God?

What daily choices do we make that move us farther from God?

---

* For the scripture passage, please use your family Bible or Fr. Nathan's *Totus Tuus*.

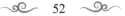

Mary was a young Jewish woman, and she considered Abraham her father in faith. Abraham's faith inspired her to be faithful. When she became pregnant with Jesus, her faith continued to grow, as she was now the Mother of the Son of God. She still believed like Abraham, but God showed her even more about who He is and who His Son is. This is why Mary is, like us, a Christian. She was the first follower of Christ.

Abraham is our Father in Faith. What was the name of Abraham's wife?

Sarah

What was the name of Abraham's son?

Isaac. (For bonus points, what was the name of Abraham's other son? Ishmael: he was born to Abraham's slave Hagar.)

Mary's faith continued to grow as she spent most of thirty years seeing Jesus every day. At the Crucifixion, Mary was given to us by Jesus as our mother in faith, and we were told to take her into our homes (John 19:25-27).

What can we do to ensure that we continue to grow deeper in faith and closer to God each and every day?

Talk with Jesus as much as possible through prayer, putting others' needs before our own, sharing our things with our siblings and friends, attending daily Mass with our parents, visiting Jesus in Adoration with our parents, monthly Confession, reading scripture daily.

Daily Pious Practice Reminder

Read and think about your bible verse.

Finish up your family consecration time by reciting the closing prayer found in Fr. Nathan's *Totus Tuus*.

Abraham, Sarah and Isaac

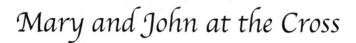

Mary and John at the Cross

Third Week
Mary at the Foot of the Cross and the Mystery of Charity

*F*aith can be either alive or dead. Faith is more than a list of things we believe in, or a list of what we can and cannot do. Our lives must be lived according to the Good News of the scriptures.

Jesus gives us the model for how to live out our faith. Jesus did many things on this earth, but three areas stand out: he taught, he healed, and he prayed. He gave his entire life to the mission given to him by the Father. Jesus offered his body on the Cross as a sacrifice for our sins. Mary stood by him through the last moments of his life. She entered into his sacrifice, offering everything she had to God. Her love for God brought her to love Jesus, and her love for Jesus on the Cross brought her to love the Apostles and the entire Church.

Which Apostles were at the Foot of the Cross with Mary?

Only John was at the foot of the Cross with Mary. It is interesting to note that John is also the only Apostle who was not martyred for the faith.

When we love someone, we feel bad when we do something that hurts that person and we try to make up for what we did wrong. Our relationship with God is the same. When we sin, we offend God; and when we repent, we wish to make up for our sins through works of charity. Charity is loving as God loves. The root of all sin is a lack of love. We must work hard to love as God loves, and Mary can help us learn to love God more as she did at the foot of the Cross.

Blessed Mother Teresa of Calcutta said that it was not so important to do great things, but to do ordinary things with great love.

Daily Pious Practice this Week

This week we offer up some small sacrifice at least three times each day. Examples include:

- Reduce the amount of time spent watching TV, reading frivolous things, or surfing the Internet.
- Do not add sugar to your coffee or tea.
- Take a less than hot shower.
- Wake up and get out of bed immediately when the alarm first goes off.

Prayer to Recite Every Day of this Week

The Memorare

Remember, O most gracious Virgin Mary, that never was it known, that anyone who fled to thy protection, implored thy help, or sought thy intercession was left unaided. Inspired by this confidence, I fly unto thee, O Virgin of virgins, my mother. To thee do I come, before thee I stand, sinful and sorrowful. O Mother of the Word Incarnate, despise not my petitions, but in thy mercy hear and answer me.

Amen.

- Traditional Catholic Prayer

First Day

Pray the Memorare

Mary, Mother at the Cross

Scripture reading from **Lamentations 3:22-32**[*]
  – *God will not abandon us; He will love us forever.*

Scripture reading from the Gospel of **John 19:25-30**
  – *Mary at the Foot of the Cross*

Mary, Mother of Mercy

If we wish to understand Mary's suffering, we need only think of how it feels when we watch a loved one suffer. When we see someone we love get sick and maybe even die, we suffer too. Our suffering may be even more intense when we watch our loved ones go through such pain, or see the sorrow of others who mourn the loss of a family member or close friend.

Have you known someone who has suffered greatly due to illness, or someone who is grieving the loss of a loved one?

Many times our own pain hurts us less than having to see those we love suffer. They may be suffering just as we are, but it adds to our pain to watch them go through hard times. Have you ever felt this way?

Mary entered into the suffering of Christ. She could have walked away and avoided watching him suffer and die on the Cross, but Mary chose to endure it all. She even consoled others present at the Crucifixion, like John and Mary

---

* For the scripture passage, please use your family Bible or Fr. Nathan's *Totus Tuus.*

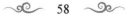

Magdalene. Surely Mary's suffering was intense. Her only son was hurt by others, and put to death while she watched. She knew he was the Lord and Savior, and that he was innocent.

When Jesus called Mary, "Woman," and gave her to John, and John to her, he told the world that she was the new "Woman," the new Eve. Mary is now the Mother of all of the members of the Church. We should turn to Mary as naturally as we would look to our own mothers. Mary looks at us through the heart of Jesus. She is so close to Him, and loves us as He loves us.

Who is the Church?

The Church on Earth (Militant or Pilgrim), the Church in Purgatory (Penitent or Suffering), and the Church in Heaven (Triumphant).

When we experience difficulties, it helps us to talk with people who have suffered in the same way. They can offer prayers and comfort to help us through our difficult time. Mary has experienced every type of suffering, and she is ready and willing to help us through our difficulties. Turn to Mary. She is your Mother: She loves you with a perfect love, and she will help you to love like God does too.

Daily Pious Practice Reminder

This week we make a small sacrifice three times a day.

Finish up your family consecration time by reciting the closing prayer found in Fr. Nathan's *Totus Tuus*.

Second Day

Pray the Memorare

Mary, Compassionate Mother

Scripture reading from the Gospel of **Luke 22:39-44***
– Not my will, but thy will be done.

What do many Christians do to respond to the Lord's request to "Rise and Pray," and perhaps make up for the Apostles' sleepiness in this passage?

Spend an hour in adoration with the Lord.

Suffering in Love

No one likes suffering; most people try to avoid it at all costs. We often pray as Jesus did in the Garden, "if possible, please let this cup (suffering) pass." But sometimes it is a little hard to unite ourselves completely to Christ and finish the prayer as he did with, "but not my will, but thy will be done."

Perhaps Jesus' prayer was asking that this cup, his suffering, be his alone. As a good son, he probably didn't want his mother to have to see him suffer and thus suffer herself. Jesus wanted to glorify God and to save us from the power of sin. He could have done it all by himself, but the Father had other plans. Mary's suffering through the passion of Jesus brought her very close to the heart of her son. She shared in his intense suffering and her heart was enlarged to love even more with the love of God.

---

* For the scripture passage, please use your family Bible or Fr. Nathan's *Totus Tuus.*

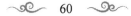

What is the value in our suffering?

No one wishes to suffer, but we will suffer in this life. It has value, and that value is to bring us closer to God our Father, so that we can love as He loves. Jesus suffered, and through his suffering he saved the world from the power of sin. St. Paul tells us that through our suffering, we make up for what is lacking in the sufferings of Christ (Colossians 1:24). This is a mystery, but it is God's plan for our salvation. Suffering is a gift from God for our own good. We can choose to accept this gift, or reject it. Jesus chose to accept it and we should too.

When we love, we forget ourselves, we go beyond our sufferings, and we are transformed by love. Love is powerful, and love is the source of our strength. We need this strength to see us through the greatest tragedies and sufferings that we will encounter in our lives. God is Love, and the more we love, the closer we are to God.

Think of a time when you have been very sad because you were sick, or someone you loved was very sick or even died.

What helped you make it through that rough time? Was it easy? Were you able to help those you love when they were sad or suffering?

Daily Pious Practice Reminder

This week we make a small sacrifice three times a day.

Finish up your family consecration time by reciting the closing prayer found in Fr. Nathan's *Totus Tuus*.

Christ Has Conquered Death

Third Day

Pray the Memorare

Mary, Most Admirable

Scripture reading from **2 Maccabees 7:20-22***
– *The Admirable Mother of seven sons*

*The mother of seven sons had to watch while her sons
were hurt by others and put to death. She could have
encouraged them to deny God and live, but instead she
praised them for staying faithful to God.*

Stabat Mater

**Is there any amount of money or any prize that would
cause you to deny God?**

*If you were threatened, would you deny God? Would
you tell any others to deny God, or would you
encourage their faithfulness?*

Our blessed Mother was filled with joy for Jesus throughout
his whole life. Even at the Cross she was joyful, for she knew
that Jesus was following the will of the Father, and she too was
following the will of the Father.

The Christian faith has always been under attack. Powerful
rulers have always felt threatened by those who put their faith
in something beyond their earthly rulers. When we put God
first, we are willing to say no to an immoral request, or to
challenge an immoral (sinful) law or action on the part of the
rulers.

---

* For the scripture passage, please use your family Bible or Fr. Nathan's *Totus Tuus*.

Mary is our source of support in those times when others try to force us to deny God and His laws. It is easy to be a Christian when things are good and there is no persecution, but when our friends go against God's laws, it becomes difficult to continue to be faithful. It is in times like these that saints stand strong, when we are able to show the greatness of putting God first in our lives.

How much would you give up for God?

Would you give up your video games, iPad, phone?
Would you give up your home, your car, your money?
At what point does your faith in God stop?

Have you ever been pressured to do something you knew was wrong?

What can you do to be prepared to choose what is right even when being pressured to do what is wrong?

We must live our faith in small ways, like praying before meals in public, to prepare for the bigger challenges to our faith. Mary, our mother, is ready and willing to help us remain faithful; and God the Father has sent the Holy Spirit to be with us and strengthen us. Do not hesitate to call on the Holy Spirit in prayer to overcome all temptations.

Daily Pious Practice Reminder

This week we make a small sacrifice three times a day.

Finish up your family consecration time by reciting the closing prayer found in Fr. Nathan's *Totus Tuus*.

Fourth Day

Pray the Memorare

Mary, Mother of Christ Crucified

Scripture Reading from the Gospel of **Luke 2:33-35***
– *Mary, your heart will be pierced by a sword.*

Scripture Reading from the Gospel of **John 19:33-37**
– *Piercing the Side of Christ*

*Legend tells us that the soldier who pierced the body
of Jesus on the Cross was named Longinus. When he
pierced Jesus' side, blood and water gushed forth,
baptizing the soldier. At that instant, Longinus
converted to the faith. He is a saint, and a statue of him
faces the main altar at St. Peter's Basilica in Rome.*

Faithful to Christ's Love

Mary is the "poorest Mother;" in the eyes of the world,
she was the most unfortunate of all mothers. She was poor
financially, having very little money. She was probably a
widow, as St. Joseph likely died sometime between when
Jesus was twelve and when his public ministry began at age
thirty. Mary's only son was tortured and put to death in the
same manner as a slave who committed a serious crime. After
the death of her only son, Mary had no one to take care of her
in the eyes of the Jewish/Roman society. She was completely
dependent on the generosity of others.

---

* For the scripture passage, please use your family Bible or Fr. Nathan's *Totus Tuus.*

What does it mean to be poor?

No extra money for toys, sweets, extra clothing. All money earned would be used to pay for your home, food, and necessary clothing.

Jesus says that the poor in spirit are blessed. Why are the poor blessed?

Because they value God and His love over all earthly possessions.

Even in poverty, she had faith that she was in God's hands and that He loved her. She trusted completely, even though she didn't understand why such bad things were happening.

Daily Pious Practice Reminder

This week we make a small sacrifice three times a day.

Finish up your family consecration time by reciting the closing prayer found in Fr. Nathan's *Totus Tuus*.

Saint Longinus

Fifth Day

Pray the Memorare

Mary, Bride of the Lamb

Scripture Reading from **Genesis 22:1-18***
– *God will provide the sacrifice.*

*Abraham is willing to give up everything to follow
God's commands, even his only son.*

Surrendering Ourselves to God

God wants us to trust Him completely, surrendering
everything we love and hold dear into His hands so that He
can use it for His glory and our good. We must obey the first
commandment and love God above all things. It is always
a danger for us to love something more than God. We must
love God more than everything, even our own family, our
spouse, or our children. God is our loving Father, and because
of Abraham's willingness to detach from all his worldly
possessions and even his only son, we have a model for how
we should love God.

Do you love God more than your possessions?

**Did God provide the Lamb as Abraham told his son Isaac
He would?**

*God did keep His word, but it took a few years for Him
to provide His lamb as a sacrifice. Jesus is the Lamb of
God who takes away the sins of the world through His
perfect sacrifice.*

---

* For the scripture passage, please use your family Bible or Fr. Nathan's *Totus Tuus.*

God wants us to love Him above all things, He wants us to serve Him, and Him alone. In a way, we are His slaves. When we value other people or things more than God, we risk becoming slaves to them. A good way to see if you are a slave to something or someone other than God is to say 'no'. For example, if you love a toy and desire to play with it all the time, see if you can say 'no' to playing with it when your parents ask you to do a chore. If you can't stop playing with it, then you may be a slave to that toy. If you can't stop surfing the Internet when you need to eat dinner, you may be a slave to the Internet. What good is saying 'yes', if you can't say 'no'?

God knows that we will only find true happiness when we say yes to Him, and love God above all things, and serve Him as a friend.

Daily Pious Practice Reminder

This week we make a small sacrifice three times a day.

Finish up your family consecration time by reciting the closing prayer found in Fr. Nathan's *Totus Tuus*.

Sixth Day

Pray the Memorare

Mary and the Glory of Christ

Scripture Reading from the Gospel of **John 17:1-5***
– *Jesus came to give glory to the Father.*

What does it mean to give glory to the Father?

We give glory to God our Father when we obey His commands (much like when we listen to our earthly parents and obey them). Our parents are proud when someone comes up to them and tells them how nice and polite their children are. When we choose to do good, we glorify God; and when people see our good works, that too gives glory to God.

Living the Victory of Love

Mary's struggles and battles were lived out with a victorious love. In every difficult situation she fought using the tools of love and not of hate. God is love and He fights evil with love. We need to love the Father as Jesus loved Him, as Mary loved Him. Mary loved the Father enough to trust Him even in the midst of the crucifixion and death of Jesus. Jesus loved the Father enough to follow God's will and give himself up to suffering and death.

What were Mary's difficulties?

Mary's most difficult moment was probably during her Son's passion and death. She probably also suffered greatly when Jesus went missing at age twelve and she

---

* For the scripture passage, please use your family Bible or Fr. Nathan's *Totus Tuus.*

*and St. Joseph could not find him for three days, and
again when her husband Joseph died.*

Mary belongs completely to the Father. We know this
because she consistently chooses to do the Father's will, at the
Annunciation; during Jesus' public ministry; and during Jesus'
passion and death. She completely gives herself to the Father,
to Jesus, and to the Holy Spirit.

St. John was a witness to Jesus and Mary's faithfulness;
John asked God to help him be faithful. Jesus gave Mary to St.
John at the foot of the Cross. Throughout his life Mary helped
St. John to endure torture and exile and still remain faithful to
God. We would be wise to do the same by taking Mary into
our home too.

How do we take Mary into our home?

*By doing a 33 day consecration to Our Lady, such as
the one in this book. Pray the Rosary daily, celebrate
Marian Feast Days, and read the scriptures and ponder
the mysteries of God.*

Daily Pious Practice Reminder

This week we make a small sacrifice three times a day.

**Finish up your family consecration time by reciting
the closing prayer found in Fr. Nathan's *Totus Tuus*.**

Seventh Day

Pray the Memorare

Mary, Morning Star

Scripture Reading from **Song of Songs 2:11-17***
 – *The dawn of a new day, winter is over and spring is here.*

I Thirst

Mother Teresa of Calcutta was inspired by the words of Christ from the Cross, "I thirst" (John 19:28). Jesus had a thirst to save the world, to defeat sin, to serve the poor, to spread the Good News, to heal the sick and brokenhearted. Jesus' words from the Cross were not a cry for water to drink but a cry for people to turn their hearts back to God.

What was Mother Teresa's ministry?

What work did she do to glorify God? She served the poorest of the poor in India. She was motivated early in her life by her mother's favorite scripture, "You did it for me." She called it the gospel on five fingers. (1-2-3-4-5: You. Did. It. For. Me.) Mother Teresa was also blessed with a vision of what God wanted her to do for Him, and she did everything she could to carry out the mission God gave her.

Do we thirst with the thirst of God? Is our mission to do the will of the Father and spread the Good News with everyone we meet? Mary thirsted for the same things Jesus thirsted for. She united her thirst with that of Jesus. Mary also allowed

---

* For the scripture passage, please use your family Bible or Fr. Nathan's *Totus Tuus.*

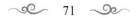

others to approach Jesus and attempt to quench his thirst, even though she knew a drink was not what he wanted. He thirsts for our love, not water!

Have you ever been thirsty? What does it feel like?

When you are thirsty, really thirsty, there is nothing in the world you can think of but getting a drink of water. You are obsessed with achieving that goal. That is what Jesus felt on the Cross. He was thirsty to be with God, and Jesus thirsted for all of us to be with God, too.

Daily Pious Practice Reminder

This week we make a small sacrifice three times a day.

Finish up your family consecration time by reciting the closing prayer found in Fr. Nathan's *Totus Tuus*.

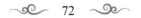

Mary and Jesus Reunited in Heaven

Fourth Week
The Gift of the Assumption

*T*he Word of God contained in scripture helps us to get to know God. St. Jerome, the Catholic priest who translated the Bible from Hebrew and Greek into Latin in the late 300s, famously said, "Ignorance of scripture is ignorance of God." God's word should inspire us and transform us. It is more than a book, it is God's love letter to us.

Did you know?

In the 300s, the language of the majority of the people in the Christian world was Latin. It was the language used by the common people. St. Jerome wanted the word of God to be accessible to everyone, so he translated it from the original languages to the language of the people. The Latin Vulgate translation is still the official translation of the Church.

Our hope is entirely in the Lord. God loves us so much that He wants us to be with Him in Heaven forever. Not only will our souls be in Heaven when we die, but at the end of time, our bodies will be resurrected just as Jesus was after three days in the tomb. God chose to give Mary a second special gift. When she was conceived, He gave her the gift of being without original sin in the Immaculate Conception; now, at the end of her life, she is brought, body and soul, to Heaven in the Assumption. Jesus rose up to Heaven body and soul at the Ascension by His own power. But, whereas Jesus ascended by His own divine power, Mary was taken up to Heaven by God's power and not her own. This is why we say that Jesus ascended and Mary was assumed.

There are two other people who are also in Heaven body and soul. Do you know who they are?

Hint: They are from the Old Testament and they spoke with Jesus at the Transfiguration.

Moses and Elijah. Moses was not allowed to enter the Promised Land. Scripture tells us that God buried him, and that no one knows the place of his burial (Deuteronomy 34:6). Since he spoke with Jesus at the Transfiguration, some early Christians believed that God took him to heaven body and soul. Elijah was taken up to heaven in a fiery chariot as Elisha watched (2 Kings 2:11). Many early Christians thought that the same thing happened with Elijah as with Moses, and that he is in Heaven body and soul as well.

We can be encouraged by Mary's Assumption, body and soul, into Heaven, because it is what God has promised us too. He gave that gift first to Mary, so that we can see He is indeed a Father who keeps His promises. We can live in the hope of God's promise and be a people of hope, and not of doubt.

Daily Pious Practice this Week

Strive to let the Light of Christ shine in our world by evangelizing others:

- Pray in public before meals with your family.

- Make time to give a reason for your hope to others. For instance, if you are asked why you have such a beautiful family, be prepared to tell them how your faith makes it possible.

- Comfort someone who is mourning and offer to pray with him and for his intentions.

- Only offer encouragement on social media, instead of criticism.

- Pay it forward – get a drink for someone when she is thirsty or pay for her lunch, perhaps a homeless person.

- Perform any of the Corporal and Spiritual Works of Mercy.

- Pray for Missionaries.

Prayer to Recite Every Day of this Week

The Hail Holy Queen

Hail Holy Queen,
Mother of mercy,
Our life, our sweetness, and our hope.
To thee do we cry, poor banished children of Eve.
To thee do we send up our sighs, mourning and weeping
In this valley of tears.
Turn then, most gracious advocate,
Thine eyes of mercy towards us.
And after this, our exile,
Show unto us the blessed fruit of thy womb, Jesus.
O clement, O loving, O sweet Virgin Mary.

V. *Pray for us O holy mother of God.*
   (This line is read by one person when the Hail Holy Queen is being recited in a group setting.)

R. *That we may be made worthy of the promises of Christ.*
   (This line is the response given by the group.)

- Traditional Catholic Prayer

First Day

Pray the Hail Holy Queen

Mary, Gate of Heaven

Scripture reading from the book of **Sirach 24:9-22***
– *Before all ages, He created me.*

Who wrote the book of Sirach?

*The book of Sirach is a letter written by a father to his
son, to prepare him for manhood. It is mostly advice
taken from the book of Proverbs. Sirach is one of the
seven books not included in most Protestant Bibles.*

Citizens of Heaven

The Blessed Virgin's life is mostly hidden from us in
sacred scripture: her birth is not recorded, neither is her death.
The Bible provides only a few glimpses: the Annunciation;
the Visitation; the wedding feast at Cana; the finding in the
Temple; a brief encounter when Jesus was preaching; during
Christ's Passion; and at Pentecost. Do you think this silence
is surprising? Mary's is not a story recorded in a history book,
but one we will all know and appreciate in Heaven.

**Do you speak more than you listen? What are some good
times to be quiet and listen rather than speak?**

Mary became the Mother of God. God, the creator of the
universe, chose to live inside one of His creatures for nine
months. He chose to be a baby and have one of His creatures
feed Him and change His diapers. No one can fully explain or

---

* For the scripture passage, please use your family Bible or Fr. Nathan's *Totus Tuus.*

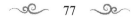

understand why God would choose to do this. What God did in Mary's life is a mystery. Only by faith can we understand and come to know the depth of Mary's life through God's eyes. A history book could never fully explain what she lived and did. She was the Mother of God - God was her child, Jesus!

Do you know anyone who has a baby?

Imagine yourself taking care of baby Jesus. How would that make you feel? It would be quite an honor and privilege to serve God in that way. This is what Mary and Joseph were called to do.

After Pentecost, we hear nothing more about Mary, but as any parent would understand, especially those who have buried a child, the longing in her heart to see her son once again would have been immense. She lived out the rest of her days desiring to be reunited with her Son in Heaven. We can be sure she prayed daily, speaking with God, the Father; with her spouse, the Holy Spirit; and with her Son, Jesus. She encouraged the early Church and St. John; and her yearning for God and for Heaven was an inspiration to all who met her.

Daily Pious Practice Reminder

This week strive to let the Light of Christ shine in our world by evangelizing others.

Finish up your family consecration time by reciting the closing prayer found in Fr. Nathan's *Totus Tuus*.

Second Day

Pray the Hail Holy Queen

Mary, Queen of All Saints

Scripture reading from **Isaiah 60:1-13 & 19***
 – *All nations shall look to Israel because God has glorified His people.*

Mary Shows us the Way

Mary lived a truly blessed life. She loved fully, never shying away from the tough times. She endured much and never complained about life being too hard, or said that she just couldn't take it anymore. We are truly living a blessed life when we go all the way to the end of what God is calling us to do and give everything we have to achieve God's plan for us.

What are some tough times you have experienced?

What kept you from giving up? If you have given up at times, what can you do differently to have the strength to not give up next time? Perhaps more prayer, more acts of daily adoration, more scripture reading.

Mary teaches us how to be fully happy. We too can offer ourselves completely to God's service every day. If we live each day as if it were our last, one day it will be true. Mary is the inspiration to give our whole life to God. She was the happiest of all people. This happiness and joy can be ours too, if we follow in her path. Mary will help and inspire us to do great things for God.

---

* For the scripture passage, please use your family Bible or Fr. Nathan's *Totus Tuus.*

What are some of the ways we can give ourselves to God?

We can offer daily sacrifices, like letting someone go before us when we walk through a door. We can be nice to someone who is not nice to us. We can choose to spend time in prayer every day, in the morning or in the evening, no matter how tired we are. We can choose to visit an elderly relative in the nursing home or play with someone no one else wants to play with.

Daily Pious Practice Reminder

This week strive to let the Light of Christ shine in our world by evangelizing others.

Finish up your family consecration time by reciting the closing prayer found in Fr. Nathan's *Totus Tuus.*

Mary, Queen Of All Saints

Third Day

Pray the Hail Holy Queen

Mary, Queen of Heaven

Scripture reading from **Psalm 45:8-15***
– *Leave behind your family and all that you love and go to the Lord.*

What is cassia?

A spice made from the bark of East Asian trees related to "true cinnamon."

Duc in Altum! – "Put out into the Deep!"

It is hard to imagine the glory that Mary entered into after her Assumption into Heaven, but we can catch a brief view of it in our faith and hope. Mary, assumed into Heaven, lives now with the Father, Son, and Holy Spirit in perfect love. Mary shows and shares with us this perfect love among the Persons of the Holy Trinity. This is the life we are all called to be a part of, and, God willing, one day we will be in Heaven too!

What does it mean to love as God loves?

It means to love no matter what, to will only what is the best for the other person and not what we may selfishly want.

Mary is our Mother too (We have the same mother as Jesus!), she loves us just as much as she loves her son, Jesus. Now that may be hard to understand, but it is true. As a good mother, she loves us, encourages us, and leads us closer to God. What is our response to this great love? St. John Paul

---

* For the scripture passage, please use your family Bible or Fr. Nathan's *Totus Tuus.*

II told us to put out into the deep, which in Latin is "Duc in Altum!" (Luke 5:4). Mary knows how difficult it is for us to leave ourselves behind and trust God so completely, but she made that choice and encourages us to do so too. Our Mother will help us to have the courage to follow God into the deep - into ever deeper love, faith, and hope in God.

How can we go deeper into Love, Faith, and Hope?

Some specific ways are spending more time in prayer, serving the poor more often, and adjusting our priorities and putting God first. Always trust that God will provide for your needs, even when you can't see how it is possible. Always be joy-filled and share that joy with the people you know. No one enjoys being around a grumpy Christian!

We meet people on a regular basis who find no joy in their Christian faith. They go to church, they pray, but there is no zeal (or excitement) in them about their faith. It is just something they do, not something they are. We need to pray for these people, and as best we can, encourage them to live their Christian faith fully. Perhaps, by our joyful, fully alive Christian faith, we will inspire them to come alive once again and regain that original faith, hope, and love that they once had for God.

How do we keep ourselves spiritually alive?

Always go deeper. Never be satisfied with where you are in your faith life. There is always more to learn about God.

How do you know when your spiritual life is dying?

Have good relationships with other Christians and ask them to let you know when they see your faith growing cold.

Daily Pious Practice Reminder

This week strive to let the Light of Christ shine in our world by evangelizing others.

Finish up your family consecration time by reciting the closing prayer found in Fr. Nathan's *Totus Tuus.*

Put out into the deep.

Fourth Day

Pray the Hail Holy Queen

Mary, Mother and Queen

Scripture Reading from **Song of Songs 3:6 - 4:1**[*]
– *Solomon's wedding procession*

What is a litter or a palanquin?

It is a carriage without wheels that slaves would carry while the king was riding in it.

Listening in Silence

Our world is full of noise. Silence is now considered something to be avoided at all costs. We have iPods, iPhones, headphones, radios, TVs, computers, etc. All of these items are meant to entertain us at all times so we don't have to endure any silence. Besides the issue of the content of the noise we fill our minds with, we also need to consider this: We need silence so we can hear the voice of God speaking to us.

What distracts you from hearing God?

Not many of Mary's words were recorded in Sacred Scripture. When she speaks, her words are very powerful and have profound meaning (the Wedding Feast at Cana, the Magnificat, the Annunciation). After Jesus and Joseph, Mary's son and husband, St. John knew her best. Although Mary didn't say much, St. John wrote quite a bit, and Mary's silent example surely inspired him.

---

[*] For the scripture passage, please use your family Bible or Fr. Nathan's *Totus Tuus*.

When we have a secret, we are silent; we keep that secret and do not utter it to anyone. Mary knows the secret of Jesus, and she tells us the secret: Live with a burning thirst to love. Jesus on the Cross told us that he thirsts. Mary heard this plea, as did St. John, and they both carried that thirst to love throughout their lives.

Do you thirst for souls?

Is this thirst the first thing in our mind? God's thirst for souls is a divine thirst that all Christians should have.

How does it feel when someone tells you a secret?

If you are like most people, it makes you feel special that someone loves and trusts you enough to share something very special with you.

Daily Pious Practice Reminder

This week strive to let the Light of Christ shine in our world by evangelizing others.

Finish up your family consecration time by reciting the closing prayer found in Fr. Nathan's *Totus Tuus*.

LISTENING IN SILENCE

Fifth Day

Pray the Hail Holy Queen

Mary, Spouse of the Holy Spirit

Scripture Reading from the Gospel of **John 17:22-26**[*]
  — Jesus gives to us everything that the Father has given to him.

How do we become one with our brothers and sisters in Christ?

We love them as God loves all of us. We wish the very best for them and desire perfect union with God for all of His children.

Docile to the Holy Spirit

What does docile mean?

It means being ready to receive instruction, submitting to someone else's control.

The Virgin Mary helps us be able to hear the Holy Spirit speaking to us. Once we can hear the Holy Spirit, then we need to become willing to allow the Holy Spirit to tell us how to act. Mary is the spouse of the Holy Spirit and thus her will is perfectly in tune with the will of the Holy Spirit. Mary is the model for becoming one heart with the Holy Spirit and allowing Him to instruct us on how to act. We are called to surrender our very lives to God and become His willing slave of love.

---

[*] For the scripture passage, please use your family Bible or Fr. Nathan's *Totus Tuus.*

When we were baptized we received gifts from the Holy Spirit, and they are strengthened in us again at Confirmation. In Isaiah 11:2 we are told that the gifts of the Holy Spirit are as follows:

1. Wisdom
2. Understanding
3. Counsel
4. Fortitude
5. Knowledge
6. Piety
7. Fear of the Lord

What is Fear of the Lord?

This is our desire not to offend the Lord, but this desire originates from our Love of God, not just out of fear in the sense of being afraid that He will punish us.

These gifts of the Holy Spirit help us to be the best Christians (followers of Christ) that we can be. The Holy Spirit freely gives us these seven gifts. It is up to us to receive them and put these gifts to good use.

Daily Pious Practice Reminder

This week strive to let the Light of Christ shine in our world by evangelizing others.

Finish up your family consecration time by reciting the closing prayer found in Fr. Nathan's *Totus Tuus*.

Sixth Day

Pray the Hail Holy Queen

Mary, Queen of the Angels

Scripture Reading from **Revelation 12:1-6***
– Jesus came to give glory to the Father.

Who is the woman clothed with the sun?

Mary, mother of Jesus. (We also see Mary as a woman clothed with the sun in the miraculous image of Our Lady of Guadalupe.)

What is a portent?

A sign or warning that something, especially something momentous or calamitous, is likely to happen.

What is a diadem?

A jeweled crown or headband worn as a symbol of sovereignty.

The Victory of Christ in Mary

Mary is the woman in the book of Revelation who is clothed with sun, with the moon beneath her feet and twelve stars around her head. Mary is very beautiful in God's eyes and in ours too. All of the beauty she possesses is there because of her love for God. She loves God so perfectly, and with so much passion, that her heart is completely united with Christ.

---

* For the scripture passage, please use your family Bible or Fr. Nathan's *Totus Tuus.*

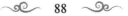

Whom do we love with all our heart?

It should be God. He is the only one we should love with our whole heart. Then, we should love our neighbor as Jesus has loved us.

Jesus is very merciful. This mercy is shown at the Last Supper when he announces that one of his apostles will betray him. Jesus doesn't say out loud the name of the apostle who betrays him in front of everyone. Jesus announces his glorification after the betrayer leaves the room.

Which Apostle betrays Jesus?

Judas. Can you name all twelve Apostles?

— Simon Peter, Andrew, James, John, Philip, Bartholomew, Thomas, Matthew, James, Jude Thaddaeus, Simon, and Judas

Jesus is glorified because Love has won and the power of sin has lost. It is a victory of love over the sin of Judas. Jesus continued to love Judas even though he knew that Judas would betray him. The example of love that Jesus gave to his disciples was to show them, and us, how to love even our enemies.

Daily Pious Practice Reminder

This week strive to let the Light of Christ shine in our world by evangelizing others.

Finish up your family consecration time by reciting the closing prayer found in Fr. Nathan's *Totus Tuus*.

Seventh Day

Pray the Hail Holy Queen

Mary, Heavenly Jerusalem

Scripture Reading from **Revelation 21:1-27**[*]
— *St. John describes the new heaven and new earth that are being presented to God. The new Jerusalem is a beautiful sight to behold, a light to the nations.*

What do think will heaven be like?

No one really knows for sure, but this passage gives us a glimpse. There will be no sorrow, no tears, and everyone will love one another as God loves each of us, only wanting the best for each other. There will be no evil, no breaking of the ten commandments, and there will be perfect friendship with everyone else. This is something we should strive for in our own homes. Think of your efforts to be good and love one another in your families as training for eternity.

Vado ad Patrem (I go to the Father)

As we conclude this week of reflection on the Assumption of Mary, body and soul, into Heaven, we ponder this reunion in Heaven. Imagine how glorious that meeting must have been, after Mary's life on this earth came to a close and she was reunited with her Son. The love she has for God is fully realized when she enters Heaven.

---

[*] For the scripture passage, please use your family Bible or Fr. Nathan's *Totus Tuus*.

How can you prepare for your entrance into Heaven?

We can strive every day to follow God's command to love Him with all our hearts.

When she was assumed into Heaven, the love that burned in her heart while on earth became glory, and Mary's soul was clothed in glorious light. Everything she endured on earth, her maternal, virginal, and suffering body, is now in Heaven. She is glorified for our sake, so that we may know that despite our limitations and failings, God can redeem us and we can be perfectly happy with Him in Heaven.

Who are you looking forward to seeing when you get to heaven?

Answers will vary, but the Lord Jesus should be first on the list.

Daily Pious Practice Reminder

This week strive to let the Light of Christ shine in our world by evangelizing others.

Finish up your family consecration time by reciting the closing prayer found in Fr. Nathan's *Totus Tuus*.

The Presentation of Mary

Fifth Week

The Presentation of Mary in the Temple - Icon of Consecration

*M*ary is our model for consecration. Today, after four weeks of preparation, we ask Mary to prepare us to surrender ourselves to Jesus just as she did. We will spend the next five days preparing for this consecration. St. Louis de Montfort gives us some practical advice on preparing for this consecration:

- Go to Confession
- Receive Communion
- Recite the act of consecration
- Offer a tribute to God to show your sorrow for past sins:
  - fasting
  - giving alms (giving money to the Church or to the poor)
  - lighting a votive candle
- Renew this consecration every year on the same date – or every month, or even daily, using this simple prayer:

"I am all yours and all I have is yours,
O dear Jesus, through Mary, your holy Mother."

Daily Pious Practice this Week

Visit Christ in the Blessed Sacrament daily.

Prayer to recite every day of this Week
Ave Maris Stella (Hail Star of the Sea)

Hail, bright star of ocean,
God's own Mother blest,
Ever sinless Virgin,
Gate of heavenly rest.

Taking that sweet Ave
Which from Gabriel came,
Peace confirm within us,
Changing Eva's name.

Break the captives' fetters,
Light on blindness pour,
All our ills expelling,
Every bliss implore.

Show thyself a Mother;
May the Word Divine,
Born for us thine Infant,
Hear our prayers through thine.

Virgin all excelling,
Mildest of the mild,
Freed from guilt, preserve us,
Pure and undefiled.

Keep our life all spotless,
Make our way secure,
Till we find in Jesus,
Joy for evermore.

Through the highest heaven
To the Almighty Three,
Father, Son and Spirit,
One same Glory be.
Amen.

- Traditional Catholic Prayer

First Day

Pray the Ave Maris Stella

Jesus, Savior of Mankind

Scripture reading from **Philippians 2:4-11 & Psalm 131:1-3***
– *Before all ages, He created me.*

Why was death on a cross considered so horrible?

*It was the form of death reserved for the worst
criminals and those who were not Roman citizens,
possibly for slaves. It was also one of the most painful
ways to die.*

Invited by the Father

The Father has shared a great secret with us and the world,
His Son. God the Father loves us so much that He gave us His
greatest gift, which is Jesus. Jesus is God's secret of Love. We
may find it hard to understand, perhaps impossible. Think of
the best gift you could possible receive and then multiply it by
100, 1000, or more. The gift of God is so much more valuable
than the greatest gift we can receive from another person.

What gifts have you received that you really loved?

*Answers will vary. Discuss how we can make sure that
we value the gifts of God more than gifts that we receive
from our friends and family.*

Jesus now gives us his own life so we may have eternal
life. Jesus gives us everything he receives from the Father. We
have been given the life and love of Jesus, all we need to do

---

* For the scripture passage, please use your family Bible or Fr. Nathan's *Totus Tuus.*

is to accept it. Sacred scripture tells us that to have life to the fullest, we must become like Jesus. St. Paul also tells us that it is no longer he who lives, but Christ who lives within him (cf. Gal 2:20). The more we become like Jesus, the more human we become, the more we become who God created us to be.

The Christian band, Mercy Me, wrote a song entitled "So Long Self." This song is a fun way to ponder what it really means to forget yourself and put on Christ.

How can you put God first and yourself second?

Serve others. Always ask the Holy Spirit what you should do in important decisions of your life.

Saint Damien of Molokai gave up everything and let Christ work through him to serve the sick and dying in a leper colony. He desired to die to himself and put on Christ. To serve in a leper colony was considered a death sentence, because the disease was so contagious and there was no cure. St. Damien died of leprosy.

Daily Pious Practice Reminder

Visit Christ in the Blessed Sacrament once per day.

Finish up your family consecration time by reciting the closing prayer found in Fr. Nathan's *Totus Tuus*.

SAINT DAMIEN OF MOLOKA'I

Second Day

Pray the Ave Maris Stella

Jesus, Our Hope

Scripture reading from **Judith 16:13-16***
– *Let all creatures serve the Lord.*

Obeying the Will of the Father

Jesus was sent by the Father to the world, and he passed on to us everything that the Father gave to him. One of the main goals of the Christian life is to forget yourself and put on Christ. When we are born, everything is about us; our world seems to revolve around us entirely. But as we grow up, we need to gradually move beyond this view, grow less selfish, and eventually become more concerned about others than ourselves.

What is the best way to think about others instead of yourself?

> *Start with little things, like washing the dishes, picking up dirty clothes off the floor, opening the door for someone - all without being asked.*

When we live according to God's plan for us, we will find the most joy and peace. God wants what is best for us. He is the perfect Father and would never give us something that would harm us. He only wants what will bring us the greatest joy. But it may happen that we do not understand how something that we can't see or don't want can be the very best

---

* For the scripture passage, please use your family Bible or Fr. Nathan's *Totus Tuus.*

thing for us. Times like that are when we most need to turn in prayer to the Father and ask for understanding, faith, and hope.

The communion of saints is the relationship we share on earth with the people who have died and gone to Heaven. But it is also a phrase we use to describe the relationship we share with fellow Christians still alive on earth. The beautiful thing about the communion of saints among Christians on earth is that each holy person is striving to follow the will of God. In order to be in Heaven with God, we must be perfectly conformed to the will of God. When we ask Mary and other saints to help us in the struggles of life here on earth, we know that we too will be able to follow the will of God.

Who is your favorite saint to pray to for help? Why?

St. Anthony is the patron saint of many things, but the one he is best known for is for finding lost things. One quick and easy prayer is "St. Anthony, St. Anthony, please come round. Something's lost and cannot be found." St. Anthony has helped many people find things that were lost. Many times these things were found in places where someone had already searched.

St. Gerard Majella is the patron saint of pregnant women.

We pray to various saints just as we ask a good friend, or someone who has been through a similar difficult situation, to pray for us. Saints are those who have run the race successfully and are with God in Heaven. They will help us perfect our prayer and ask God on our behalf to help us through our times of trial.

When your prayers are answered, be sure thank God and the saint whom you asked to intercede on your behalf.

Daily Pious Practice Reminder

Visit Christ in the Blessed Sacrament once per day.

Finish up your family consecration time by reciting the closing prayer found in Fr. Nathan's *Totus Tuus*.

Saint Joseph and Jesus

©2015 R. Miller

Third Day

Pray the Ave Maris Stella

Abba, Father!

Scripture reading from **Romans 11:33 & 12:2***

What does Abba mean?

*It is the Hebrew word meaning Daddy. It is a very
personal way of addressing your Father.*

Worshiping the Father in Spirit and Truth

Jesus offers adoration to the Father by his obedience to the
Father's plans for him. Since we as Christians are seeking to
be like Jesus, we too offer adoration to the Father by following
His plan for our lives.

In our daily lives, we are offered many paths, many
options, and many choices. Some of these choices are very
attractive, but ultimately lead us away from Christ instead of
closer to Him.

**What are some examples of choices that appear to be good,
but when we look closer, we see that they lead us away from
God?**

*Eating ice cream in moderation is okay, but eating too
much ice cream is committing the sin of gluttony.*

What is Gluttony?

*When we eat way too much just for the sake of bodily
pleasure, rather than respecting that food is intended to*

---

* For the scripture passage, please use your family Bible or Fr. Nathan's *Totus Tuus.*

nourish our bodies and help us to celebrate important things. Gluttony is sinful because it shows a lack of self control with regard to food.

We are made for eternity, and each choice we make in our daily lives leads us closer to God or further away. We should always seek to grow closer to God in everything we do. We must ask the Holy Spirit every day how we can grow closer to God in the simple and ordinary daily things we do. St. Therese of Lisieux believed that everyone can reach holiness by doing little things each day. The Church agreed with her so much that she was declared a Doctor of the Church.

Daily Pious Practice Reminder

Visit Christ in the Blessed Sacrament once per day.

Finish up your family consecration time by reciting the closing prayer found in Fr. Nathan's *Totus Tuus*.

Saint Therese
of Lisieux

© 2015 R. Millar

Fourth Day

Pray the Ave Maris Stella

Jesus, Eternal Wisdom of the Father

Scripture Reading from **Revelation 12:10-14***
— *The evil one has been defeated by the blood of the lamb.*

Witness to Hope

We are the witnesses to hope in this world. We may be the only "Gospel" that anyone will ever read. St. Teresa of Avila said, "Christ has no body now but yours." This is true, we are the hands and feet of Jesus here on earth: It is our responsibility to serve not only the physical needs of people, but their spiritual needs as well. Every person we come into contact with could be looking to us for hope. Our hope is in Christ; how well do our actions and our lives show that hope?

What are some things we can do to show our hope in the Lord?

> *Daily prayers, treating others with respect, attending Mass regularly, our priorities in life (God first, spouse second, children third, then all others).*

Mary is the ultimate witness to hope. Even when she was faced with profound suffering in her life, she still had hope in the Lord, and surrendered her only son and all of her life to His service. She knew that God was faithful and that He would not betray her trust. We too should keep our eyes fixed on Heaven, on God's promise of eternal life. It is keeping our focus on eternal things that will help us through this valley of tears. This

---

* For the scripture passage, please use your family Bible or Fr. Nathan's *Totus Tuus.*

life on earth is short, but it is our training ground for eternity; it is our opportunity to choose to love God first and to help others to do the same. Our witness to hope may help someone else have stronger faith and hope in God, or it may help someone who has no hope to find the Lord for the first time.

Daily Pious Practice Reminder

Visit Christ in the Blessed Sacrament once per day.

Finish up your family consecration time by reciting the closing prayer found in Fr. Nathan's *Totus Tuus*.

Pope Saint John Paul II

Fifth Day

Pray the Ave Maris Stella

Jesus, Son of the Father

Scripture Reading from **Revelation 14:1-7***

The 144,000 had the Father's name written on their foreheads. When do we have something written on our foreheads?

At Baptism (and again at Confirmation), our heads are anointed with chrism and marked with the sign of the Cross. Our foreheads are marked with ashes on Ash Wednesday.

Follow the Lamb with Mary

In order for the Lamb, Jesus, to be most perfectly in our lives, we must ask the Lamb's mother, Mary, to be part of our lives as well. Mary is the perfect example of how to follow Jesus, because she is present from the Annunciation through the Passion, death, and Resurrection of Jesus. There are no sufferings that she avoids; she embraces all that the Father sends to her. Mary lived for Jesus alone, and she received perfect joy from God.

Mary perfectly followed Christ through his mission in this world. She was faithful to God through the good times and the bad times, in sickness and in health, for richer and for poorer. She dedicated her life to helping God accomplish His plans for the world through her son, Jesus.

---

* For the scripture passage, please use your family Bible or Fr. Nathan's *Totus Tuus*.

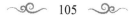

Where do we also hear the words above (through good times and bad etc)?

During a wedding ceremony, the love of God is what we practice through the sacrament of Christian Marriage. Marriage is a training ground for loving as God loves.

When did the Holy Family have riches?

When they received gold from the Wise Men.

When did the Holy Family experience sickness?

When Joseph died, and during the Passion of Jesus.

To follow Christ, the Lamb of God, we try to do what God wants us to do in all things. God is perfect love and His ways are higher than our ways. He knows us best, He knows what will bring us true joy and not just temporary pleasures. If we rely on Him and follow His will, we too will find the perfect joy that Mary found.

How can we know what God wants us to do?

Read scripture, pray, frequent reception of the Sacraments, and by being quiet and listening for God's voice.

What can we do to show love to others?

Open the door for someone, clean the kitchen when no one has asked. Do nice things for others, tell your parents and grandparents you love them.

Daily Pious Practice Reminder

Visit Christ in the Blessed Sacrament once per day.

Finish up your family consecration time by reciting the closing prayer found in Fr. Nathan's *Totus Tuus*.

Follow the Lamb with Mary

Family Consecration Prayer

I, _____,
*a sorrowful sinner, renew today the
vows of my Baptism. I reject Satan
and all his empty promises and
desire to follow Jesus Christ more
than I did yesterday.*

*Mary, I give you my heart. Please
help me love Jesus more. Help my
heart to burn with thirst for love
and for souls as Jesus did on the Cross. Keep my heart
close to your pure Heart that I may love Jesus and other
Christians with the love of God.*

*Mary, I give myself totally to you: everything I have and
everything I will do in my life. Please use me in whatever
way you desire. Let me be your servant to bring the
greatest possible glory to God. If I fall into sin, please
lead me back to Jesus.*

*Wash me in the blood and water that flow from the pierced
side of Christ, and help me to always seek the love and
mercy of Jesus. Mary, with you as my example, I unite
myself with Jesus as He offers Himself in the Spirit to the
Father for the life of the world. Amen.*

Signature: _____

Date: _____

Living out Your Consecration

Congratulations! Now that all the members of your family have consecrated themselves to Jesus, through Mary, what can you do as a family to live out that consecration? Hopefully, this time of preparation has been fruitful for your family and each member of your family is closer to our Blessed Mother and her Son as a result of the past 34 days of prayer and reflection. We pray that your family has seen the value of time spent each day in prayer with the other members of the family.

Here are some practical ways in which your family can continue to grow closer to the Lord daily by living out your consecration:

- Pray the Family Rosary every evening (could be done at the same time as you have set aside for the daily consecration reflections)
  - Your Holy Family will soon be making available a *Family Rosary Companion*. This guide will help you to delve deeper into the mysteries of the rosary, and make the beauty of each mystery accessible to your entire family.
- Celebrate feast days in a special way–go to Mass, special dinner, a party with other families
- Continue to perform the daily pious practices that were done each week during the preparation
  - Daily acts of Adoration
  - Daily Scripture reading
  - Offering up a small sacrifice
  - Evangelize others
  - Visit Christ in the Blessed Sacrament

- Pray the Angelus daily (during Easter, the Regina Caeli)
- Build a community of faith in your neighborhood
  - Invite another family to dinner
  - Invite someone who doesn't have family locally to dinner or to spend special holy days with your family
  - Organize a family Rosary night or family Stations of the Cross
  - Organize a Family Fun Day (FFD)* at your parish or in your community
  - Organize a Teen Shenanigans (TS) at your parish or in your community
- Be a family of service
  - Visit a local nursing home
  - Volunteer as a family at your parish (parish festival, community service projects, or start a new ministry for families (see FFD and TS above))
  - Home-bound ministry–taking communion to those in nursing homes or shut-ins; food pantry; hospitality ministry
  - Visit your extended family for no special reason, just to be with them and perhaps do small household maintenance items

---

* For more details on the Family Fun Day and Teen Shenanigans's Programs please see the Resources Section at the end of this book

Your Holy Family Resources

Raising a Holy Family can be a daunting task, but you don't have to do it alone. Denae and I founded Your Holy Family Ministries to provide families with practical help to lead their families to heaven. We know many families who have overcome enormous challenges to raise a holy family.

Our family has been blessed with being a part of a vibrant parish and a very strong community of families. This community didn't just happen by accident, we and other families in the area worked hard to create communities centered around Christ. In our quest for resources to enhance our family life and our local community, we have encountered many great programs, conferences, and camps. Below is a list of various resources that may help you as well:

- www.YourHolyFamily.com - articles on family life and a calendar of family related events around the country.

- The Apostolate for Family Consecration and Catholic Family Land - www.afc.com

    - Outstanding Catechetical resources, and a family summer camp that can't be beat.

- Midwest Catholic Family Conference

    - Programs for every member of the family, outstanding speakers, and programs for the kids run by religious brothers and sisters.

    - Held the first weekend of August in Wichita, KS

    - www.catholicfamilyconference.org

- Fullness of Truth Conferences

    - Regional Catholic Conferences in the Southwest

    - www.FullnessOfTruth.org

Retreats for the Family

A weekend event to retreat from the world and its pressures; renew and reclaim your family. We Pray, Play, and Rest together as a family and build community with other families. While there are many good conferences and retreats that minister to the individual members of the family, we recognize that there is a real need today to heal the family unit. We seek to provide an opportunity for families to rediscover each other and heal divisions that may prevent them from living out what John Paul II describes as a communion of persons. We seek to reunite the family through inspirational talks on family life, family centered projects and activities, family games and sports, and family friendly entertainment.

"Come away by yourselves to a secluded place and rest a while." Mark 6:31

If you would like to offer a family retreat at your parish, school, or in your community, we offer assistance with planning from start to finish, as well as facilitating the retreat weekend. Contact us and we can discuss how we can help you put on an unforgettable weekend experience for the families in your community. We have run very successful retreats for families ranging in size from 125 up to 400 attendees.

Our non-profit conducts yearly retreats for the family in Texas. Donations to our ministry go towards offsetting the costs of running these retreats so that families of all sizes can afford to attend these very powerful family building weekends.

More at: www.YourHolyFamily.com/retreats

Workshops on Family Life

Workshops on Family Life are one day events designed for parents who want to learn practical tools to build up the Domestic Church. Workshops go in-depth into topics that will help parents navigate the sometimes rough waters of family life.

Often, family life consists of transporting children to various activities outside the home, homework, school activities, work, household chores, etc. Family life can devolve into a home shared by individuals who happen to be related to each other. The family should be much more than this. It was designed to be a refuge from the world, a source of joy, and a sign of true love. As St. John Paul II said in *Familiaris Consortio*, the mission of the family is to Guard, Reveal, and Communicate love.

Workshop Topics include:

- Setting Family Priorities
- Implementing Family prayer in your home
- Respect within the family
- Keeping your kids Catholic
- How to get perfect behavior from your children at Mass
- Dating which preserves your child's purity
- Maintaining good channels of communication with your children even through the adolescent years
- Family Vacations

More at: www.YourHolyFamily.com/workshops

Family Fun Day & Teen Shenanigans

A Family Fun Day is an opportunity to take a half day to rest from our busy schedules. The day starts with a potluck lunch for fellowship, followed by faith formation for parents; meanwhile the teens and young adults play sports, cards, and board games with the younger kids.

The middle of the afternoon is devoted to a family activity related to the topic of the family fun day talks. Next, the parents play with their kids and the teens will have their own faith formation time. The day concludes with a family rosary honoring our Blessed Mother. The Family Fun Day is an occasion to show your family that you value being with them above all the other commitments that we have throughout the week.

An important part of the Family Fun Day is nurturing our relationship with our teens. Since this can be challenging if we have both teens and younger children, we have developed a companion event to the Family Fun Days. Teen Shenanigans takes parents and teens on a journey to strengthen their relationship through playing and sharing their faith. Teen Shenanigans is a chance for us to reward our teens with a special night out with one or both parents. A time to eat some food, play cards, dice or board games, and share our faith in a a fun and relaxed setting.

More at: www.YourHolyFamily.com/family-fun-days

Community of St. John Programs

Marian Faith Network - www.MarianFaithNetwork.com

Video and audio presentations on Mary by members of the Community of St. John for young people wanting to live in the spirit of total consecration.

Copies of Fr. Nathan's Totus Tuus Consecration Book may be purchased at the Marian Faith Network website.

Eagle Eye Ministries - www.EagleEyeMinistries.org

Mission: To form, unite, and inspire young Catholics for the new evangelization by deepening their relationship with Jesus Christ, through prayer, study, culture, and community.

We provide in-depth formation in the Christian life for young people, by: bringing them to an authentic encounter with Christ in Faith; providing rigorous intellectual formation in the light of God's word and the philosophy of Aristotle; fostering authentic expressions of human culture; and offering them the experience of community which will allow real friendships and support on the path to holiness. We not only want to inspire our participants to do great things with their lives and offer them the formation that makes it possible, but we also want to provide them with the resources they need in order to find their unique place in the Church.

66619320R00071

Made in the USA
Charleston, SC
23 January 2017